THE BOOK OF
STANDING
OUT

TRAVELS THROUGH THE INNER
WORLD OF FREELANCE TRANSLATION

ANDREW MORRIS

ISBN: 1500924342
ISBN-13: 978-1500924348

DEDICATION

For Brigitte

CONTENTS

WHY I READ
STANDING OUT...

I was fortunate to stumble across *Standing Out* just as I was embarking on my freelance career. It quickly became a cherished source of motivating tips and intelligent, thought-provoking conversation. There are tons of pages about the whats, whens and hows on the surface of translation. *Standing Out* is about the whys and hows that motivate us at a deeper level. Andrew Morris has created a venue in which intelligent, thoughtful members of our profession engage in (yes, cordial!) dialogue and banter.

> *Dr Ellen Yutzy Glebe*
> *German > English translator*
> *Germany*

It offers a reminder, from a variety of perspectives, that your career is just that – yours – and as such, you have completely free rein to define what 'success' means, in your own terms and based on your individual interests and personal circumstances. *Standing Out* is compact and incisive and gives me pause for thought in my working day and new insights for my subconscious to go to work on!

> *Zoe Bishop-Beal*
> *French>English translator*
> UK

Coffee and the musings of *Standing Out* are a good way to start out my workday. Although a few olives and almonds once in a while would be welcome.

> *Hildegard Klein-Bodenheimer*
> *English > German Translator Germany*

Because he stands out.

> *Dennis Brice*
> *Swedish > English translator*
> *Sweden*

Where else can you get deep philosophical musings, useful ideas, entertaining banter and terrible puns – all in one place?

> *Gill McKay*
> *German & French > English translator*
> *Germany*

I read *Standing Out* because it opens up a new, better way of thinking to my mind, not just related to translation but to life in general.

> *Heather McCrae*
> *German > English translator*
> *Germany*

To my mind, it is essential that translators develop and expand from the very core of their being their own philosophy on all matters relating to translation specifically and life in general. This pool of dedicated, constructive thought is what sustains us in our work. By honing our skills tangentially thus, the daily achievement of excellence in translation. How wonderfully refreshing it is for me to see a very different, but kindred, spirit that is Andrew Morris sharing his thoughts on *Standing Out* page! What's more, *Standing Out* engages a lively bunch of fellow translators no less talented to do the same. We all have so much productive fun. Long may it last!

> *Allison Wright*
> *German, French, Portuguese>English translator*
> *Portugal*

I read *Standing Out* at gun point (beats washing the dishes anyway). No, really! I actually read it as I always find a piece of advice or a witty comment that helps me stay on track.

João Correia
English > Portuguese translator
Portugal

I read *Standing Out* because it inspires me, it makes me think outside the box regarding my career and it also makes me think about the importance of olives.

Maria João Trindade
English > Portuguese translator
England

I usually follow *Standing Out* because we have several ideas/ethics/'rules' in common and it is always a pleasure reading the posts and the commentaries that follow them. Great minds think alike, that's what they say, right?

Rita Menezes
English & French > Portuguese translator
Portugal

I read *Standing Out* for fellowship and information.

Hélène Sinany
English & Russian > French translator
USA

For me, reading *Standing Out* is pure reflection. I think of the many things that I do, want to do and dream of doing. It helps me realise that having a fulfilling and enjoyable job is possible.

> *Anna Barbosa*
> *Portuguese>English translator*
> *Brazil*

I read *Standing Out* on a daily basis because it reminds me of why I love working in the language sector, even (or maybe especially) if I had a bad working day myself.

> *Andrea Busse*
> *English & French > German translator*
> *Germany*

Although getting started with a job you love is somewhat easy in the morning, I find it even more stimulating after a visit to *Standing Out*.

The topics for discussion are extremely varied, sometimes complex, always interesting and providing food for thought. Oh and incidentally, Andrew Morris' sense of humour is a blessing on rainy days!

> *Ode Laforge*
> *English > French translator*
> *France*

I always look forward to clicking on the latest *Standing Out* post when I turn on my computer in the morning because it is just like that first cup of fresh brew which opens up my senses for a day full of new promises with renewed energy and hope for a productive day of creative translation work:-)!

> *Virginia K. Fox*
> *English > French Translator*
> *USA*

ACKNOWLEDGMENTS

My thanks go first of all to Ana da Silva, whose chance remark one afternoon opened my eyes to the whole online world of translation fora of which I had been blisslessly unaware. One thing then led to another on the long journey that culminated in the publication of this book.

Along that route stood a number of excellent colleagues who encouraged, helped, advised and inspired me and in some cases presented me with undreamed of opportunities: Andrew Bell, Nicole Y. Adams, Eve Lindemuth Bodieux, Anne Diamantidis, Siegfried Armbruster, Marta Stelmaszak, Lucy Brooks, Gala Gil Amat, Anne de Freyman, Rachel Malcolm, Iwan Davies, Helene Tammik for the careful proofreading. Eleanor Toal for the invaluable marketing advice, Frédéric de Souza for the photography, Chris Matthews for the design and last but not least my brother Jon Tregenna, whose idea it was to turn my musings into a book.

Above all my special thanks go to those who have visited the *Standing Out* page on a daily basis, contributing hugely through their comments, counter-arguments, lucid perceptions and unfailing enthusiasm. They are too numerous to mention here, but they know who they are. I will remain eternally indebted. Without them this book would never have come about.

ABOUT THE AUTHOR

Andrew Morris has been a freelance translator since 2009, working from French into English and specialising in the arts, culture and tourism. He runs a small but perfectly formed translation studio by the name of Morristraduction.[1]

His previous job experience includes language teaching, teacher training, part-time journalism, working as a waiter in a pizzeria (thankfully only for six months as a student) and playing the piano in a psychiatric hospital. But not in that order.

Other equally colourful experiences include two years spent living in a hut in a remote valley in North-East Africa, playing saxophone in a concert on New York's Broadway with a Bangladeshi folk-rock band and the day he met his partner Brigitte when they discovered they were both reading the same book, on a train between Paris and Rouen. The title? *'Le Livre des Coincidences'*.

He has worked long-term in ten countries, visited over 50, and learned more languages than he can now remember. He now lives, writes and translates in Provence in the South of France.

---

1 www.morristraduction.com

FOREWORD

The miscellaneous musings that make up this book initially appeared in random order on my *Standing Out* page, popping up in response to haphazard events in my daily life as a translator, things I'd read and comments and questions from readers.

For the purposes of coherence and readability, they have been grouped here into six chapters, even though some of the individual pieces could possibly belong in more than one place.

Chapter One - *Hearts and Minds* is all about attitude. It examines the vital area of what we bring to our working lives above and beyond our basic technical competence. And it explores the perceptions, emotions, beliefs and behaviours that mark our professional careers and arguably exercise a deep and lasting impact on what we achieve and how far we get.

Chapter Two - *The Vision Thing* takes a broader look at the world of translation and some of the apparent truisms by which so many freelance translators live. It assesses and in some cases questions what has often become received wisdom in translation circles.

Chapter Three - *In your Hands* explores the extent to which we as professionals can and must engage with, craft and even create the circumstances in which we work. Its starting point is the notion of autonomy - that we are responsible for our professional lives and can play a much larger part in shaping them than we often think.

Chapter Four - *The Perfect Likeness* is centred round the idea of authenticity - each of us has a unique contribution to make to the world of translation, and one of our roles is to sculpt a working life for ourselves that most authentically resembles our own individual identity and values, helping us move ever closer to a fulfilling and enjoyable professional experience.

Chapter Five - *The Entrepreneur's Apprentice* offers a collection of anecdotes, tips and reflections from the wordface on how we deal with our clients and colleagues - demonstrating how some of the theories touched on in earlier chapters can work out in practice.

Chapter Six - *Loose Ends* hoovers up all those miscellaneous and whimsical pieces that didn't fit into any of the other sections.

Many of the pieces are followed by selected comments left on my page by regular readers. These have been left unedited and add a welcome richness and texture to the debate. Comments have not been included for those earlier pieces first posted on the Watercooler forum and then transferred to *Standing Out*.

I hope you enjoy reading and reflecting on these pieces as much as I have enjoyed writing and collating them.

And that they prove as beneficial to you as they have been to me.

Andrew Morris
Provence
2014

1 HEARTS AND MINDS

Take ten competent translators with a year's experience, in the same city, all in the face of a single national economic climate.

Give them all 15,000 euros, a brand new laptop, access to the Internet, a menagerie of CAT tools, business cards, a website, a catalogue of trade fairs, the entire paraphernalia.

Shower them with books on improving their marketing, their rates and every tip and trick in the translexicon.

Then leave them to get on with things for a year.

Come back and compare their results. The outcomes will differ wildly.

The ones who have struggled will blame it all on the economy, the technology, the evil bastards out there, the way things are going to hell in a handcart.

And they will gather together and endorse each other's views heartily, amid much drowning of sorrows and gnashing of teeth.

The ones who thrive will have a different view.

Adept at transformation, they will know that what really counts is what's inside, not outside: thoughts, emotions, attitudes, values, beliefs. All stuff that can be examined, worked on, changed.

It's a hundred times more challenging and a thousand times more rewarding than blaming everyone and everything else.

And it starts inside your head and your heart. That's where you need to look.

If you're to keep your head above water as a freelancer, of course you need to be competent, master the tools, be accessible and reasonably organised. We can all agree on that. If you can't actually translate ideas from one language into another, and get it done in time, you should try something else: pastry chef, landscape gardener, astronaut or circus acrobat.

But competence can only take you so far. It's not even a very glowing notion in English. Try describing Placido Domingo as a 'competent' singer or Jose Mourinho as a 'competent' football manager and see how flattered they are.

Competence is the bare minimum, and it accounts for about 25% of what you can achieve. It will no doubt ensure that you survive as a translator.

But if all you do is survive, you'll sooner or later find yourself standing still. Worse, you'll end up moving slowly backwards as the world moves ahead. Because there's no space, no mental room for openness and creativity when you're in the survival zone.

Survival is an emergency mode in which all your mindspace is taken up in defending what you have. Creativity goes out of the window. Our ancestors in caves didn't get much painting done on the days when there were storms howling, fires raging or predators prowling around…

Which is why our aim should be not to survive but to thrive.

What fascinates me is why some people, including translators of course, go so much further than just getting by and begin to truly fulfil their potential.

That's where the remaining 75% comes in.

Cinda Evans Brooks *Your statement: 'But if all you do is survive, you'll sooner or later find yourself standing still. Worse, you'll end up moving slowly backwards as the world moves ahead. Because there's no space, no mental room for openness and creativity when you're in the survival zone' is possibly the best call to maintain a quality program of CPD I have heard for some time. So many translators simply survive on competence.*

Miranda Joubioux *I'm with you on the passion side of things. You need motivation, stimulation, inspiration or whatever you like to call it, to carry on day in day out. I didn't actually realise that I was passionate about what I do until I took on a student for her work experience. She thanked me for communicating the passion I have to her. The more I do this job the more the passion grows. Some might say how can you get passionate about the workings of a boat or a building or a lawn mower, for that matter? Well it's the art of crafting words that I love so much and it drives me on every single day. I have moments when I lose confidence, but never the passion.*

So if our technical competence accounts for 25% of our success, what does the other 75% consist of?

Think about those who attain 90% or 100% of what they have the potential to achieve.

If I look around at the people I see thriving in our little microcosm, my conclusion is this: it's all about their mental and emotional approach. That's their 75%. How they perceive and react to what happens to them, make decisions, project their personality, act creatively and build relationships...

Put simply, it's the 75% that optimises (or conversely, undermines) the 25%.

If your predominant ways of interacting with clients, colleagues and the world in general are based on perseverance, resilience, determination, certainty, joy and enthusiasm (irrespective of whether or not you're an extrovert) you will begin to exploit your full potential: opening doors, making connections you never even knew existed, seizing possibilities and moving towards fulfilling your true capacity.

But if your 75% is founded on defensiveness, protection, anger, suspicion, guilt, hesitation, frustration and mistrust, your potential will be severely hampered. You'll be able to do your job alright and you may well have bread on the table and enough money in your pocket (if not in the bank). But chances are, you'll also be beset by nagging fears about cash-flow, famine and the future. And not just now and again, but on an almost permanent basis.

And of course sooner or later, you'll lash out at agencies, the system, the whole damn world.

In that mode, you're working against yourself, whether you realise it or not, hammering away at your own 25% with a 75% mallet.

Most people don't grasp this of course, and find it much easier to blame everything on the world around them.

So in short, the extent of our achievements above and beyond survival is primarily the consequence of our own attitudes and behaviour.

But is it possible to make the shift from surviving to thriving?

I think it is.

All you have to do is change your mind.

Miranda Joubioux *There are pessimists and optimists among us. It's the glass half full/empty syndrome. If there was a key to turning from many years of pessimism (often inbred) to optimism then I think someone would have found it by now. The fact that you keep looking is a sign that you are a true optimist. I agree that attitude is everything and that anyone is capable of turning things around, but they have to really want to. Some people become complacent about their situation and make no effort to seek change for fear of what it might entail.*

Standing Out *I agree wholeheartedly. I have come across a few such keys in my recent explorations… but as you say they're not easy to integrate or apply. And it takes commitment. And courage, because you're right, fear paralyses and keeps us exactly where we are. And it's also just a little bit comfortable, enabling us to shift the responsibility outwards.*

Miranda Joubioux *That last comment is so true!*

Marie Karlsson *I agree that attitudes and behaviour are essential aspects. Can I ask how you define a 'thriving' translator? Do you mean an individual translator who considers herself/himself to earn more than what it takes to make a living, i.e. has the possibility to spend and/or save an amount every month after the regular bills have been paid?*

Do you mean a fully booked work schedule? Or are you talking about time? The luxury of having the amount of free time that you desire, because of very efficient project management and maximisation of your workflow, using your CATs in an optimal way, which makes it possible to earn as much as possible in the shortest possible time? Perhaps a combination of these?

How did I come up with the figures, you may well ask your-selves, that led to the 75%/25% distinction?

Well, a couple of recent lectures, conversations with a friend who's a neuroscientist and another who's a chiropractor, some reading and a bit of intuition based on experience.

But what if all of them and I are entirely wrong and competence in fact accounts for 95% of success and your mindset is just 5%?

I've heard people suggest pretty much that. 'What makes people successful, young Morris,' they say, 'is simply the quality of their work. Their craft, their technique, their qualifications and just possibly their Linkedin profile. Now run along with all this selfy-helpy mumbo-jumbo clap-trap about attitudes, there's a good lad.'

Well for a start, if it were just that, there would be far more thriving translators… around 95% of all of us would be tap-dancing to work and whistling on our way to the bank.

Because there's enough work for everyone out there. And because I'm pretty sure you're all splendidly competent. But looking around, that tap-dancing quotient is not quite the impression I'm getting.

Correct me if I'm wrong.

Maria João *You're not. I was one of the best at university, I finished my course 7 years ago and I'm still surviving instead of thriving. I don't know if it's my attitude, but it's definitely not my competence.*

Standing Out *These are questions only we can answer, to ourselves. And it often goes deeper than how we're feeling today, this week, or even this year. I think our brains and emotions operate in circuits which are so entrenched that we hardly know they're holding us back, even if we* feel *positive. Part of the learning I'm pursuing is about simple ways of repro-gramming the system. Without the use of coffee. Or mushrooms.*

Hildegard Klein-Bodenheimer *A while ago, I read somewhere an article about being financially successful with translation work. Something along the lines, if you really want to earn X amount (Like in 5 years I want to earn half a million a year) you can do it. And if you don't succeed you don't really want to be successful. First I was very much opposed to this view but somehow it stuck in my head. And slowly I am thinking, maybe* *it's not so wrong. Maybe most of us don't want it badly enough. Maybe that is what holds so many translators back.*

Elina Sellgren *Your post really got me thinking about my own situation, what is my experience and does it resonate with your ideas (you really have a talent for this!) I think my wake-up call was last autumn when after my summer holiday in August, everything was dead. I had barely any jobs for about a month and a half. It wasn't a financial crisis for me because I have savings but it really gave me a good scare. I spent all that free time on sending out applications, working on my profile on different websites, reading up on people's ideas about how to succeed as a freelance translator (and I bought Corinne [McKay]'s book too). I got my company name in July and I had to look at my finances analytically and in an organised manner.*

I realised I only had 2 major clients who provided 90% of my income! I got rid of one of them by the end of the year (though I still take the occasional job if they agree on my new, improved rates). One is still with me but I also have a slew of clients. In October, I started to receive more job offers than I could handle... And the new clients are not the ones I sent applications to... they just approached me out of the blue saying my profile on x is interesting and they'd like to collaborate! Would this have happened if I had been buried under all the work from the 2 big clients? Don't think so! So I think sometimes you just need a good kick in the butt!

So how *do* we define a thriving translator?

For me the answer is quite simple and rather Buddhist in orientation. I define a translator as thriving if they are living most of the time in a state of non-suffering.

On a number of levels:

- They earn as much money as they need to be comfortable, however much that is, plus a little bit left over for olives (substitute treat of choice).
- They also have the equipment they need to get their job done, even though there may always be new-fangled programs and kit just out of reach.
- Their work space is pleasant and conducive to concentration and calm.
- They have as much work as they want to be doing, with at least some ability to pick and choose, and are dealing most of the time with the kinds of texts they find inspiring.
- They feel connected to a community rather than isolated.
- They are moving ahead and learning new things every week, not changing the world, but deriving a sense of fulfilment and progress, with realisable goals ahead along their own professional path.
- And their non-suffering extends beyond the material and intellectual realms to the people they work with and for, so that they are not mired in relationships based on hostility but feel like respected partners.

- They feel they are generally in control of their lives, and not subject to the whims of others, even though the rare exception may arise.
- They are in a good place (in their own eyes) physically and spiritually.
- They accept that their situation entails, and will always entail, a balance of benefits and challenges.
- And their predominant state of mind is gratitude for the way things are, while remaining excited about the way things *could* be in the months ahead.

As you can see, it's not too ambitious a list. ☺

The amounts of money and work involved, the text types and the client profiles will clearly vary from individual to individual.

In other words, no two thriving translators are the same. There are also the über-thrivers of course, who take off and spiral into the stratosphere, but that's not necessarily a path everyone wants or needs to follow. For now, I'd stick with the simpler definition above…

Miranda Joubioux *You can have a professional situation that is all that you say and still have external influences that bring you down. Thriving is an art form. It has to work in all areas of your life and for many of us it doesn't, because we don't get the balance right even though we spend a lot of our time trying. This in itself is probably the greatest challenge.*

Allison Wright *Agree with Miranda Joubioux that thriving does depend on how you deal with the curve balls life throws at you. And yes, Andrew, sometimes the impact of these missiles can be forceful indeed.*

Standing Out *My focus here is clearly on professional life. But yes, of course, factors from other spheres of life can impact seriously on our professional wellbeing.*

Otherwise I'd have said 'a thriving human being'. But that's a few steps down the line...

On paper, you tick all the boxes. The clients you have are delightful and you just love translating. What's more, your pink and purple pens are all neatly lined up on your desk, your website is all spruced up and your designer business cards are lovely to the touch. You can translate well enough (feedback has proved that) and your office is comfortable.

But it's still not working out for you. And you're frustrated as to why.

Could this be an opportunity to look beyond the confines of the professional domain?

One thinker[1] I have read and listened to a great deal divides life into seven spheres:

- vocational (which is what I've been writing about up to now)

---

1 John Demartini

- family/relationships
- spiritual (which might be yoga, meditation or whatever)
- intellectual
- financial
- physical/health
- social

For each of us, these will come in a specific order, but for most people reading this page, the vocational will be at least among their top three priorities: it's where you're most organised, where you direct your attention, what inspires you, what you think and talk about.

One sign that the vocational sphere is important for you (yes, you!) is because you're reading this right now, when you could be out eating an ice cream, twerking, chasing butterflies or robbing a bank.

Your top three spheres may also include family of course, or sport (physical), or reading (intellectual), yoga or meditation (spiritual) or socialising… Work may come second or third, but it'll be up there somewhere.

However, if *any* three, two or in some cases even one of the seven spheres, even those lower down your personal hierarchy, are seriously off-kilter, then it's going to be difficult to thrive fully in the professional domain. The borders between the seven spheres are far from watertight… If, for example, you're in a dysfunctional relationship, or have serious health or weight problems, or are overdrawn at the bank or extremely lonely.

Which is why, ultimately, only a holistic view can lead to a thriving life beyond and including the workplace.

It's usually pretty obvious which of the seven spheres needs attention when we look at our own lives. All emotional disquiet is nothing other than feedback: not the sign of the immutable way things will be for the rest of your life, but an invitation to transform stuff - either the situation or your perspective.

And yes, before you ask, I have been there. It's far too personal to write about here, but I have hurtled all the way down to the very bottom. However, what happened when I got there led to a change in just about everything in my life. It wasn't neat, linear or clear at the time, but it is now, looking back.

Sometimes we have to switch a zoom lens for a wide angle to get the whole picture.

Gill McKay *Very much agree - as far as I'm concerned, 'success' in only some of these spheres is not success. Though I am twerking whilst reading this.*

Hildegard Klein-Bodenheimer *Great food for thought. We often forget that all parts of our lives influence (sometimes mess with) each other. Good to care for all of them, mind, body and soul.*

Claire Wilmin *Yep, work isn't everything, thriving is a general balance of life that can only be controlled by each individual according to what makes them tick. ☺ For example I thrive by also teaching and doing a fair amount of sport and training. They keep me sane because I know I need to get away from that computer screen at times!*

Miranda Joubioux *I have learnt through kinesiology that our bodies tell us things when our lives are unbalanced, but that we rarely ever listen. The body is an amazing thing.*

Aside from that I would like to say that although we have control over many aspects of our lives (particularly work) we do not always have control over everything. In fact I would even go to say that it would not be normal to have full control. Some things have to run their course and that course may be over many years. Attitude will always help you through, but you have to remember that some life experiences can be very debilitating. When people are unhappy everything can look like a miserable mountain to climb. This frame of mind can creep into every aspect of your life. I suspect there are many translators out there with issues in their lives. It is not for us to judge them. However, helping people become aware of the overall picture can only be a good thing. I hate to hear some of the petty lecturing that goes on in our circles. (Let's be clear, you are not included) It achieves little. What is important is create the awareness that everyone can raise their sights a little and make progress. It's not about entering a battle, but about creating an overall picture that helps you use your intelligence wisely and finding the determination to bring about change. I hasten to say that this applies to me as much as anyone else.

I had to smile recently to see myself associated in a couple of posts with 'Positive Thinking'. Time to knock that one on the 'ed, methinks.

I do happen to be a fairly positive person… I was just born that way. And my friends always say that when I was a kid, I would always bounce back up, no matter HOW long they held my head underwater.

But the positive thinking industry (see Barbara Ehrenreich's masterly exposé '*Smile or Die*') turns me right off. Life isn't about saying 'This is the best of all possible worlds' 50 times into the mirror every morning, or furiously denying the existence of difficulties and surrounding yourself with pink balloons. It's about equilibrium, and that means welcoming both the upbeat moments *and* the problems with open arms.

And recognising that every phenomenon is not only impermanent but double-edged. Every positive situation has a downside and every negative one has an upside.

The whole *Standing Out* phenomenon has been a wonderful development for me, but of course it has meant lots of extra work, time and effort in an already hectic day too. It's also elicited some criticism and the occasional broadside from people I've never even heard of. I knew and know that, and I take it in my stride.

Similarly, a client who doesn't pay, or a text which turns into a nightmare edit, is feedback, and contains vital lessons and learning… for next time. It's about deposits, signed documents, checking before you accept a job, and so on. Ultimately that very client will improve your operation.

As long as you learn.

These experiences are never pleasant as you go through them, but the problem contains the solution, if you look hard enough.

And it's usually in your hands.

Too much positivity and you spiral off into euphoria, out of the reach even of those who love you. Too much negativity and you sink into depression, equally cut off. In neither state are you much good to the world or to yourself.

So enough already, as my imaginary Brooklyn-based great-grandmother would have said.

I'm not a positivist. More of a pogativist, or a nesitivist. Or just a balancist.

I just opened a document that I used when I first started offering coaching sessions, and which I sent to people as a prompt for their thinking.

I was proud of it the day I wrote it. It had some pretty colours.

Today I am astonished at its naiveté.

I wrote it all of.... oh... six months ago.

Your first reaction when you look back at something you have written, created (say a website) or even (though less frequently) translated, is often to wince. I looked at my first ever home-made website recently (that was 5 years ago, admittedly) and found it worthy of a primary school. And yet at the time I thought it was the smartest thing on earth.

But the upside of these sentiments is of course that they show how far and how fast you've moved on.

So cringe by all means. But for no more than 30 seconds. Then celebrate.

And if the things we wrote 2 years ago make us cringe, that also means perhaps that the truths we hold as rock-solid today might themselves appear naive in 2 years' time.

One more reason never to take ourselves too seriously.

SJB Translations *The way I look at it, there are lasting truths and there is fashion. The hard thing is telling them apart without hindsight, but if you can do it you're really going somewhere.*

For every bad agency you name, I can name a good one. For every unscrupulous taskmaster, I can name a great boss.

For every cruel cartoon PM, I can name a friendly one.

It's a game that could (and does) go on forever. But what does it prove? That you're right? That I'm right? That we're both wrong?

No, it just proves that we're looking at the same world... but through different eyes.

Look back at the past, as a professional and as a person. Every single event in your life falls into one of two categories:

- The things you feel you can't say 'Thank you' for. They become your baggage.

- The things you can say 'Thank you' for. They become your fuel.

Changing your perspective so that events from the first category become part of the second is not always easy. But it's possible, and vital.

Having more fuel than baggage will get you far further in life.

But you're allowed a toothbrush and a change of socks all the same.

One way of understanding what happens to our minds during empty inbox days and other trials and tribulations of the translator's life...

At such times, the standard response is to retreat into insecurity, frustration and feelings of powerlessness and even anger. Your left brain takes over, the part that got you out of a fix back in the cave days when there were beasties lurking outside. You become analytical, cautious, reliant only on what you know and what's worked in the past. There's no room for philosophising: you have just two options, fight or flight.

One by one you can hear the sound of doors shutting all along the corridor of your mind.

And where's your creative right brain during that time? The one you used to use to paint symbols and images on the walls of the cave? Realising it's not being called upon, it heads down the fire escape off to a hammock on a tropical island, sipping pina coladas and humming calypsos. Because when you retreat into left brain mode, when you're driven by fear, annoyance and worry, your right brain has nothing much to do.

It's the worst possible state in which to make any major decisions.

However, when you put your fears to one side and start to think about what the lessons can be (there's always one somewhere), and look for active ways out rather than just crumpling, your right brain flies home and hits the tarmac faster than you can say 'Business class'.

Inside its suitcase is everything you need: creativity, imagination, intuition and play: all the keys to re-open those doors...

It's during those more open-minded, creative moments that you come up with the right ideas, meet the right people, see the right opportunities, make the right connections. Where you get those flashes of sudden insight.

Why do you think the greatest scientists get their best inspiration outside the intense atmosphere of the lab? Because they stop turning round and round the same problem and let their artistic side out to play. In a dream, down the pub, trudging through the fallen leaves of an autumn park.

At which point your left brain, far from heading off for a break at the North Pole, comes into its own – to structure and plan, to stop the dream floating off into the sky, to organise and give it grounding and shape.

It's not easy to switch either brain hemisphere on or off at will of course. Although they found a few ingenious ways back in the 60s...

But knowing that both halves are there and what they're meant to do is a useful first step.

Peter Bowen *Or necessity is the mother of invention*

Standing Out *Indeed so, but only if you look at it the right way. Otherwise it becomes the mother of yet more necessity...*

Hildegard Klein-Bodenheimer *Thanks for a great post. I am giving my left brain a day off and will see what the right one is capable of doing.*

This week, a single remark from a colleague made me decide to totally change the way I run my business. It led to a few significant transformations in just one day. The colleague had no idea what they'd sparked off.

And the funny thing is, the moment I decided, new work began to flow in that exactly mirrored that decision. But that's another story, for another day.

I've always believed that just about anything anyone says to you is a lesson in disguise.

Okay, perhaps not the words 'Tickets please', uttered on a train (although even they can be a pretty good lesson if you've attempted to dodge the fare). But pretty much everything else.

So you take a chance remark, and you build a theory on it. You dig deep and interpret it for what it might be saying to you.

It's hard work. Never forget that. But the rewards make it all worthwhile.

But, I hear you cry, what happens if you dig up the wrong interpretation? You've only got your intuition and instincts to go on, and they may well have led you into hot water or down a blind alley in the past.

Well, there's only one way to find out. Do it. You may dig up a can of worms. Or maybe a crock of gold. Just keep learning the lessons as you go. You can always change again as the realities unfold.

Your life is the best teacher you'll ever have. But how good a learner are you?

Alison Hughes *I often have a few things on the back-burner which materialise after a single remark that just kicks my brain into gear.*

Politicians, even mid-term, are often asked to explain what they believe in and what they stand for. I'm not a politician, and luckily I don't have to account to anyone, as I didn't make any election promises and no hands were shaken or babies kissed in the making of this book.

But I do often feel called to account to *myself*, and answer the question 'What is this *Standing Out* for?' Such musings are usually prompted when I get a lovely piece of feedback from a reader in some distant corner of the world, which suggests that the impact frequently extends far beyond what I thought or expected...

So here's a new angle on what this is all about.

Beyond linguistic brilliance, translation talent, technical wizardry and marketing magic, (all of which are of course essential) there is another dimension required if we are to become translators who are not only successful and fulfilled but who also have peace of mind. (Remember that for the Stoics of Ancient Greece and Rome, the ideal state of mind was not happiness, but tranquillity).

And that is the cultivation of an approach based on certain values, attitudes and beliefs. Openness, curiosity, tolerance, equanimity, clarity, flexibility, balance, humanity and love.

But as a book I once read long ago said, 'the greatest of these is love'.

When I look back over this last year since I first set foot in the online world of translation, I realise that all the wonderful things that have happened are very little to do with objectives, plans and strategies.

And everything to do with people.

I made no ten-point lists, 6-month forecasts, three-columned whatevers to begin with…. All I did was open up to suggestions made by others who entered my field of vision, most of whom I'd never heard of on the day they popped up in my inbox or on the phone.

Almost every event was someone else's brainchild: just about the only thing that was purely my idea was *Standing Out* itself.

But while I can't claim any credit for the initiatives, I claim 1,000% credit for the response.

We are all constantly surrounded by opportunities, whether we realise it or not. So open up, make yourself available, and once you hit a certain frame of mind, you will draw towards you the people you need to move you on.

I can guarantee that.

A tale of two brains

We all know about the two hemispheres of the brain, where the left brain is about strategy, language and planning and tends to draw on the security of what we know, whereas the right brain is about creativity, imagination, play and leaping into the unknown.

We often stay in left-brain mode simply because it's what we're familiar with. It's like the comfort of an old armchair at home rather than risking the perils of travel to more exotic climes.

Although the act of translation is itself in many ways creative, our approach to the profession usually favours the left hemisphere. Hence the profusion of advice on the mechanical, pragmatic side: lists, tools and strategies: 10 ways of doing X, 20 top tips on how to achieve Y.

So much so that we may have entire periods in which we lose touch with our adventurous, intuitive capacities. Apart from in our dreams, when we finally let down our guard...

But there are plenty of ways to be imaginative in our working lives: in the way we express ourselves in our websites, logos and blogs, the way we organise our space and time, the way we approach and deal with our clients (both agencies and direct) and each other, and the way we perceive and respond to opportunities and challenges, to name but a few.

The world of translation as a playground. Discuss.

In fact we all have rich experience of right-brain living to draw on. It's where we spent the entire first decade of our lives.

Before our education tried its best to drum it out of us.

Every problem that pops up in our lives as translators hides a gift. It may not always be pleasant and we may not always want it. A bit like those embarrassing presents at Christmas time, the purple socks, the orange tie, the Donny Osmond album bought by a well-meaning aunt. But it's all feedback, if we're willing to look at where the lesson lies and turn it into an opportunity to grow.

However, every apparently positive situation also has a price to pay. Increasing your array of direct clients, for example, certainly involves more income and excitement, but also entails far greater risks and responsibilities. And it's a price you have to be happy to pay.

So there's no such thing as a problem without an upside and no luck, no progress without challenge.

But let's face it, some challenges are more enticing than others.

There is the challenge, for example, of coping with an empty inbox four days in a row. Or of doing work that doesn't inspire you. Or fending off bottom-feeders.

Or conversely, the challenge of an inbox that's bursting to capacity, which entails taking on responsibility, longer hours, juggling skills worthy of a circus artist, demands on your availability (including on weekends), dealing with more clients, financial management gymnastics, and generally having to shift up a gear.

Think of them as backwards or forwards challenges. Or push and pull challenges.

Don't know about you, but I know which kind I prefer...

And yes, we need to make a choice at some stage. Things are always moving on. Just look at where you were three years ago. And in a changing world, you either move ahead or you move backwards.

The idea of standing still is a pure illusion.

At the moment a problem strikes, the upside may seem very far away, just as the downside may seem remote at the moment a bit of good news pops up.

Like the two separate rails under your feet as you stand on a railway line...

But the further away we move from the point that is now, the less polarised the two sides become, whether we are looking back or ahead, until the point where they join.

I've trained myself to see the positive side and the challenge immediately and indivisibly, as part of the same event, rather than having to go off in search for them and reconcile them.

I think I'm getting there. At least I'm on the right track...

Hang on a minute, I hear you cry, it's easy to be assertive with agencies and clients when there's plenty of work coming in, there are olives on the table, and you're relatively established...

But which came first, the confidence or the clients?

It's the old, eternal question.

As we have seen, competence precedes both. But I know quite a few competent people with a shortage of clients.

Of course, it's certainly true that every new client engenders greater confidence, which brings in new opportunities.

But right back at the beginning, when there were no clients at all, what then?

Back then there was nothing but a bucketful of attitude. And two drops of hope.

No doubt you know this tale of Socrates at the gates of Athens....

A traveller approaches and asks: 'I'm thinking about moving to Athens. What's it like to live here?'

Socrates asks the man what his life was like in his previous home city. The man answers that it was awful. He says that the people were untrustworthy and he had no friends, only enemies.

Socrates frowns and says, 'Unfortunately, you'll find Athens to be just the same.'

Later that day, a second traveller approaches Socrates and asks the same question: 'What's it like to live in Athens?'

Socrates again asks the person what life was like in the place they had previously lived in. They say: 'In my last city everyone was open-minded and generous. They all worked together and helped each other out.'

Socrates says: 'Luckily, you'll find Athens to be just the same.'

But what happens when a would-be translator approaches Socrates and asks what the world of translation is like?

Allison Wright *Socrates takes a rare moment to look a little undignified in his toga and have a good old belly laugh. That's where the saying, 'You've got to be joking' comes from.*

Standing Out *That's right. Or he says 'Don't bother mate, there's more money in philosophy...'*

Picture a busy street in your capital city, wherever you are reading this. Imagine how it feels on a late Saturday afternoon, full of movement, traffic, bustling shoppers, shouts, mobile conversations and laughter as people spill on to the streets from cinemas, cafes and restaurants. Now look around at all the language you can see. You're a translator, so you take in all the words. Notices in shop windows, posters on walls, leaflets thrust into your hand selling everything from pizzas to religion, neon signs flashing above, street signs, a man with a sandwich board, a passing bus festooned with a colourful advert.

It's a kaleidoscopic information overload, but buried amongst those thousands of messages are the ones that could potentially change your life, in ways that range from coming across a new music group that will form your personal soundtrack for the next two years, to learning about a book or a talk that will transform your entire outlook.

Let's transfer the city street metaphor to our lives as translators. Like most people reading this book, I get dozens of emails per day. In my case they range from offers of work, applications from translators, new texts, requests for quotes, adverts and spam. Then there is the welter of words on the social fora, with hundreds of busy people behind their keyboards clamouring to be heard. Plus the real conversations you may have with colleagues or family members about your work. Add to that the actual texts you are working on and, although I've never counted, you could safely say the number of words and therefore messages that cross your field of vision in a given day runs into the tens of thousands. And who knows, in there, buried and perhaps camouflaged, could be *exactly* the words you need to take you to the next stage of your development.

I will never forget that it was a single off-hand remark by a colleague that first made me visit the Facebook forum known as the Watercooler.

I could so easily have ignored it.

But I didn't... and everything that's happened since, from the *Standing Out* page to my work with the Alexandria Project, Nicole Y. Adams and the *Bright Side*, the ITI blog and the masterclass at the ITI conference, my attendance at both the ATA conference and a summer school in Canada, plus a project with ECPD Webinars, not to mention many rewarding friendships, can all be traced back to a single throwaway remark.

Even writing those words, I'm aware of the enormity of what they imply.

Now clearly you can't go rushing off after every firefly impulse or you'd never get any work done. But between being pulled every which way several times a day and doing nothing, there is a huge gap, with many carefully graded steps along the route. So of course you need to filter all of the different stimuli in terms of where you are right now and where you want to be.

The more you know yourself and act in accordance with your deepest priorities, the more you will both recognise and react constructively to those signs.

It's like walking down an endless corridor with countless doors in different colours. Some will open to reveal blank walls. Others will be chutes which take you tumbling back down to the basement while others still can be gateways to the rest of your life. But which are which? Your instinct, intuition and judgement will play a key part...

But even before you get to sorting out what's right and what's not, you need to keep your mind alert and your curiosity and childlike wonder intact.

And your eyes wide open.

First published on the Alexandria Project Website[2].

---

2 http://alexandria-translation-resources.com/

2 THE VISION THING

There's a fair amount of victim culture in our little world of translation, between the evil ghost of Machine Translation hovering in the wings, the rapacious agencies, (oh and don't get me started on the Big Guys), the constant lament about the crowded market place, and the ever-present refrain about how fees are being driven down.

My goodness, it's carnage out there. So much so that it's possible to throw your hands up and say 'With things that bad, what can a translator possibly do to survive?' If you're that way inclined, that is.

But I'm not that way inclined. And my answer to the question is simple. 'Everything'.

When I started out I'd never heard of multi-language vendors, I wasn't familiar with the term machine translation, and I certainly knew nothing about the lurking monsters and the clouds hanging over the industry, if some of the prophets of doom are to believed. I simply began by working on what I had to do, creating my own space, in a tiny village in rural France, and doing it as well as I could, and the rest gradually fell into place. And it's not over yet…. I'm just getting into my stride.

The fact is that your life as a translator is in your hands, not anyone else's and certainly not 'the industry's'. Realising this is about making the shift from victim to agent, from someone at the mercy of 'market forces' to someone who decides that from now on, they are in control, and they will call the shots. It's about understanding that your own professional world, with all its ups and downs, is nothing but your own creation.

Always assuming, of course, that you're actually good at what you do, and that you haven't missed your real vocation, somewhere along your journey, which was to become a vet, concert cellist or master baker of cupcakes.

So rather than trying to change the whole world, if you work on your own little patch of it and become the best translator you can be, showing yourself in the best possible light, and pushing yourself to grow, you will stand out. And that's a promise. Not only that, you will thrive and watch your professional life begin to develop in ways you never even imagined...

How am I so sure of this? Because it's exactly what happened to me in the five years since I first became a translator. And I've seen it mirrored in countless other colleagues since.

Now don't get me wrong. Getting ahead and standing out from the crowd doesn't mean trampling on other people. There's room for everyone, all standing out from each other. It simply means finding your unique niche and letting your own individuality shine through.

So forget about who else is out there and what they're up to: just work on yourself as a professional practitioner and the rest will follow. When your own vision is stronger than the other hectoring, doubting or complaining voices around, and when you do what inspires you, in a way that inspires you (or, as someone once said, 'You tap-dance to work'), then you will soon see that people can't wait to get what you have.

Of course along the way there will be challenges, obstacles and experiences that may initially appear as mistakes or even failures, but are in fact the most valuable feedback you can have. It's part of the game. Who wants an easy life anyway?

(First published on the Alexandria Project Website[3])

A credo for this wordy world of ours...

I believe that none of the myriad translators who publish online or on paper has a monopoly on the truth...

I believe that individual translators are perfectly capable of visiting a whole number of fora and blogs and taking out whatever they need to help them on their journey at that point in time. Each person on a different pathway, with a different history and destination.

I believe that no translator needs to or can be told what to think.

I believe that newbie translators are not newbie human beings.

I believe that everyone is capable of looking around and seeing that life, especially professional life, has its ups and downs.

---

3   http://alexandria-translation-resources.com/

I believe that the more perspectives there are feeding into the debate, the better. There are no 'sides', just a wealth of viewpoints. Sides are for primary school.

I believe that whenever a new publication or book comes about, it only adds to the richness of what is available. It is not the 'truth'. Beware any person that makes that claim.

And I believe that this diversity is something to celebrate. Finally, I believe that after that immense intellectual effort I am entitled to at least one chocolate biscuit.

Every time somebody sounds off online about a client or agency committing this or that unspeakable evil, somewhere, softly, a door closes.

Every time everyone piles in and says 'Yeah! The bastards!' and takes the perpetrators out, another few slam shut, not least within people's minds...

Every time a dogmatic position is adopted, insinuations fly, offence is taken or egos are ruffled, you can hear the sound of keys turning in locks.

One of the purposes of this book is to throw those doors open wide.

On the ups and downs in the mind of a translator. A thought: I reckon we can all agree that there are:

a) terrible agencies
b) appalling rates
c) wheeler-dealers
d) hucksters and jokers
e) disorganised PMs
f) unrealistic clients
g) overblown expectations
h) and yes, mediocre translators out there.

It's not really a matter of debate, it's just a fact.

But here's another fact. Every time we bang on about those, our gaze is drawn downwards, our energies are pulled towards the lowest common denominator, and it brings out the worst in everyone. The frustration, the tensions and the anger. Whole fora go round and round in endless circles nagging at these issues.

And the irony is of course that all that hot air changes precisely nothing. And never has done. Because little good ever comes out of anger. It just reduces your field of vision to a tiny focus and shuts down creativity and intuition.

So do we just close our eyes?

No.

Me, I'd rather look up. Find the best examples of translators, inspiring business leaders, example-setters and innovative practitioners out there, and try to be more like them. I'd rather spend my precious time reading what *they* have to say...

They may be harder to find, it may require more effort, but it's ultimately a much better way to move ahead.

So keep looking upwards. Just don't get a stiff neck.

A quick thought for the day, between two paragraphs of a lovely text on a very nice spa resort (where I would *so* like to be right now...)

Creative translation isn't about whether you can speak and read a foreign language (although that helps).

It's above all about whether you can write well in your own language.

Now that I'm back from the Quebec course on translating for high-level clients and have had time to reflect, how do I feel? Well, a bit like someone who started out climbing a mountain five years ago, then graduated to walking briskly up a hill, and after that began to enjoy strolling up a gentle incline, confident that the summit was within reach, perhaps just round the corner.

Only to turn that corner and find another mountain staring me in the face.

Just like when I play the piano at home, and am quite pleased with the music I produce. And then I go to a concert and see what can be done by a virtuoso and suddenly see my fingers for the pudgy little pink sponges they are.

Indeed, for all the hype surrounding some of the big names in our profession, often obsessively and exclusively focused on their earning power, what I glimpsed in some of these sessions was nothing short of translation genius, distilled.

And I want a piece of that.

Ah well, time to start climbing again.

At a recent workshop I heard a presenter say that in his team, the key question he always asks when reviewing the work of others is not 'Is this a good translation?' but 'Is this a good piece of communication?'

In his view, the end reader has less than zero interest in the source text. The only real criterion of success is 'Does this work as a standalone text?'

We attract the clients we deserve.

And we attract exactly those experiences we need to move forward.

Whether we learn from them or not is up to no-one but us.

Here's a great quote from another of my heroes, the most excellent Stephen Fry, to ponder over your morning coffee.

'We are not nouns, we are verbs. I am not a thing - an actor, a writer - I am a person who does things - I write, I act - and I never know what I'm going to do next. I think you can be imprisoned if you think of yourself as a noun.'

So if you're not a translator, what three verbs are you?

Neil McKay *I've always taken a certain pleasure in baffling people who ask 'what do you do?' by saying things like: 'I travel, hike, bike, drink red wine, play music'. 'Oh, sorry, you mean what is my job? That's just what I do to earn money to do the things that actually define me'.*

In translation, one of the most important and yet hardest things to do is to tear yourself away from the source text. So strong is the glue...and the fear of stepping away.

Take a sentence like this:

'Après des études de biologie et des cours d'art dramatique Jean Dupont débute sa carrière au théâtre.'

You can play around with this however you want:

1. 'After graduating in biology and attending drama school, JD began his acting career.'

Hmm, not bad, accurate enough, but a bit flat. Even if the opening sentence itself is a bit unadventurous in the source text, I'd like something spicier...

2. 'JD studied both biology and drama before taking to the stage.'

Bit better, bit more natural. Some nuances lost. Some ambiguity in there ('biology and drama'?)

etc. etc

What I tend to do these days is ask myself: 'If this was about me, what would I say if I was writing this from scratch?'

I then take a giant (metaphorical) pair of scissors, cut up the source text, throw the bits up in the air, and start again...

3. 'JP studied first biology and then theatre before he began to tread the boards.'

I could go on and refine with each fresh look, but at least the third sentence has a little more of a flourish. It's what I'd want to write about myself if it was my life I was describing.

Of course, if it was my career, I wouldn't start with such a boring sentence anyway. I'd probably want to say...

'Back in the biology lab, JP little knew that...' or 'The theatre lights were a far cry from...' or 'It's funny the turnings life can take...'

But there are limits to how many liberties you can take... And limits to how much time you can spend on a single sentence.

Are agencies bad or good? Both.

Are freelancers bad or good? Both.

Why, because there's nothing in our profession that's wholly bad nor good.

Word for the day: Manichaeism (adj. Manichaean). A belief in the struggle between a good, spiritual world of light, and an evil, material world of darkness.

Think George W. Bush or Ronald Reagan. But they're not alone.

It first emerged in the 3rd century CE, but still seems to be going strong in certain sections of translatordom.

I was speaking to a translator recently who said 'I just do tourism, arts, luxury goods, and gastronomy texts. I wish I had a specialism.'

Believe me, I've seen enough mediocre translations in precisely these areas to know that they *are* a specialism...

They may not be as specialist in terms of *content* as microbiology or patents (although any long translation on a cathedral, a top-end watch or a grand piano manufacturer is going to involve a fair amount of expertise and research), but in terms of the writing skills required and the ability to put ideas together fluently and engagingly, they are very much a speciality field.

And one that is far more sparsely populated than you might think.

Years ago in another life I was a teacher trainer, regularly giving presentations to audiences of teachers worldwide for Oxford University Press. From Tripoli to Hong Kong and from Zurich to Moscow, I would fly in, mike up, get the PowerPoint on the screen, talk to anything up to 600 teachers gathered in a hotel or conference centre, and usually try to end with a funny story to go out on a high note.

Job done, it was often a quick lunch and off to the plane. I could have written a book on the world's airports, as I got to see at least one new one a week.

But just occasionally, I had the chance to stay on a couple of days, and was shown around the city.

It happened once in Ljubljana, the capital of Slovenia. It was in December 2003 and the streets were cloaked in silent snow. The black spires rose above the city and the winter markets were full of fur-hatted people stamping their feet to keep warm, their breath frosting up in the evening air.

My local hosts had invited me to dinner in a wonderful old-fashioned restaurant. Yellowing photographs from decades past on the walls, candles flickering on the table, reassuringly heavy silverware in your hand. Faces around the table glowing with warmth as the snow continued to dance outside the window.

And a waiter, whose name I forget now, but whose skill was astonishing - a blend of charm, expert knowledge of the menu and wines, practical deftness and humour, combined with that inestimable ability to know when to be discreet and when to step forward with a timely and witty observation.

He was a truly outstanding professional and he taught me a valuable lesson... that it doesn't matter what you do in life: if you do it with inspiration, passion and excellence, people will never forget you.

On tilting at windmills...[4]

In five years' full-time work as a translator, I've never met, seen or even heard from a bottom-feeder (if you don't count spam). I don't think I'd know one if I walked into one. And if I did, I'd say 'Hi' and 'Bye' within about two seconds. Because funnily enough, in my world, it's me who gets to decide who I work with.

Which is to say that their existence (which I don't deny) neither impinges on mine nor bothers me in the slightest possible way.

I must be a) lucky b) blind or c) stupid

Or maybe it's just that:

d) I'm freelance.

On a similar note, here's an interesting word for the day: paedomorphism, or juvenilisation - the process whereby we regress into childlike behaviours and attitudes.

Above all, turning freelance is about being an adult, no longer looking to parent figures to protect us from big bad monsters but assuming full responsibility, enjoying the rights of a grown-up and also facing the ups and downs with as much equanimity as we can muster.

---

4   Common phrase meaning to attack imaginary enemies, based on Cervantes' 17th century *novel El ingenioso hidalgo don Quijote de la Mancha*, or *Don Quixote* in English)

To me, whinging at length online is wrong not just because it's 'negative' and because 'clients might see it'. Those are superficial reasons. The real harm is that it sends us spinning back into a state where we demand to be rescued and protected, validated by others and told we're right. As opposed to going out and changing the way we see and do stuff.

I'm not hugely religious myself, but I do enjoy the poetry of the venerable old books, and this verse in particular:

'When I was a child, I spake as a child, I understood as a child, I thought as a child: but when I became a man, I put away childish things.'

Cora Hackwith *Well said. You learn from any experience, including and perhaps especially the bad ones. Learn and move forward.*

Standing Out *I'm all for posts that go: 'This is what happened, and this is what I did to get round it'. That's quite instructive. I'm much less interested in posts that say 'Can you BELIEVE what the bastards have done this time???'*

Let's return to the subject of venting, which intrigues me. Of course I've described it as whinging above, but for the purposes of this piece we'll adopt a more neutral, less value-laden word.

Does it do us any good? Does it serve a purpose?

I've been in work situations way back in my past where I vented a great deal, compounded by the fact that my ex-wife was in the same teaching job. So we could vent to the power of two. We vented at the language school, which was indeed very badly run, we vented on the metro and tram as they wound through the city of Prague and we carried on venting when we got home. Then we probably vented some more before falling asleep, all vented out, only to dream of all the things we forgot to vent about during the day...

We'd probably have won a gold medal in the Olympic mixed doubles venting.

But my conclusion looking back is that it actually achieved nothing. Zilch. Nada but a constant churning feeling inside and probably all kinds of unknown effects on our health at the time.

It certainly changed nothing in the work place. The problem only ended when we did the right thing and left after just a year.

So what's your opinion? To vent or not to vent? (Quite apart from the wisdom or otherwise of doing so in a highly visible public place. Here I'm talking only about the notion itself).

There will always be an endless supply of venters of course, and nothing we write here will change that. But it's interesting to unpack the issue and look at it from a new point of view.

In English, it's common to say 'A problem shared is a problem halved'.

But is it? Or is it in fact doubled?

We are told 'It's good to vent' and that 'suppressing' is bad for you. We never consider the third option: dissolving.

Indeed, we have a whole battery of phrases to describe this pastime: 'get it off your chest', 'unburden yourself' 'let off some steam', 'air your grievances'.

Note how the latter two curiously involve the idea of air, as does the word vent itself of course.

But is it all in fact just hot air, full of sound and fury, signifying nothing and achieving still less?

Simon Ash *I think it depends whether you're venting at someone who will reinforce and multiply your irritation, which is gratifying in the short term, or at someone who will gently absorb some of the steam, condense it and a little while later spray some cool refreshing water on your aggravation.*

Heather Jennifer McCrae *I vented silently or on my own most of my life, these days I open my mouth more often when something annoys me. But these days, I also think twice about whether it is actually worth it or if there is a different approach. I've also realised that I need to check my own glass house before casting any stones. Reminding myself of all the good things in and around my life also helps to decrease frustration, so here is a tip for everyone: List all the things that are good in your life at least once a day, you will actually be amazed how long that list can get.*

Peter Bowen *I have learned the wisdom of dissolving, as you put it, or taking it in my stride/rising above it, but wisdom and practice do not always coincide with the beauty of the principle. I rarely actually vent but when I do it is certainly necessary as my head would surely explode otherwise. Sport is*

another great outlet. Squash, cycling, whatever takes your fancy. But ulti-
mately the only solution is to resolve the source of the frustration/irritation.
Or at least try to do so….

Allison Wright *To me, venting (as experienced by my 'angry young*
woman' self many years ago) springs from a sense of desperation and power-
lessness at 'the injustice of it all'.

These days, I question why, as supposedly autonomous human beings
with all the human rights in the world, people who vent place themselves in
a position of desperation and powerlessness - and why people (I just love the
wide, sweeping sin of generalisation I am committing here!) do not negotiate
a better position, or vantage point for themselves to obviate the 'necessity' for
venting in the first place.

Chiara Di Benedetto Brown *I think there's a difference between*
venting, which implies that at some point the material to be vented is ex-
hausted and then you are empty and free of it and can move onto more posi-
tive things, and wallowing, where you continually produce material, not to
be divested of it, but to somehow feed off of it. I think a lot of times we may
not even know we are doing this, it's a dangerous vortex.

I attended a 'translation slam' in which prominent translators Grant Hamilton and Chris Durban gave their contrasting
and occasionally conflicting versions of a single source text.

Both enjoyable and humbling to watch two top professionals tackle the subject.

Interesting to see how, at this level, you leave the source way behind, basically rewriting the whole thing, throwing sentences around, breaking them down, beefing up concepts, inventing titles, getting rid of subtitles, generally 'zapping it up a bit' and even in one case adding a final slogan as a flourish.

The goal? To write 'consistently compelling English'.

(So easy when you see the finished translations of course). It's all about developing a certain elasticity and daring, and constantly coming back to what you might write if you were not translating but writing the text from scratch.

Or adopting 'an irreverent approach to the source text'.

Standing Out is all for irreverence.

What did I translate this week? Wrong question.

Ask me what I did.

I helped a communications agency director look great in front of her big international client.

I enabled a few families in far-flung places to pore over a brochure and choose their next holiday.

I regaled some museum-goers with an enjoyable learning experience in a foreign city.

I gave an academic a hand in getting his paper published. Human things.

The words are just a bridge. Look to the other side.

3 IN YOUR HANDS

How many of you knew this about the word 'freelance'? The term was first used by Sir Walter Scott (1771–1832) in Ivanhoe (1820) to describe a 'mediaeval mercenary warrior' or 'free-lance' (indicating that the lance is not sworn to any lord's services, not that the lance is available free of charge).

It changed to a figurative noun around the 1860s and was recognised as a verb in 1903 by authorities in etymology such as the Oxford English Dictionary. Only in modern times has the term morphed from a noun (a freelance) into an adjective (a freelance journalist), a verb (a journalist who freelances) and an adverb (she worked freelance), as well as into the noun 'freelancer'.

Not sworn to any lord's services, but certainly not available free of charge. I think I like that (says he, conveniently glossing over the 'mediaeval mercenary' bit...)

But remember, ' 'When I use a word,' Humpty Dumpty said, in rather a scornful tone, 'it means just what I choose it to mean — neither more nor less.' '

Recently I phoned round a few of the local tourist offices, who all have robust communications budgets here in the South of France. As I called one, an employee positively grabbed the phone out of the answerer's hand and said 'We need a translator!' (A response that usually only happens in dreams).

Put the phone down in a state of euphoria. Sent an email response, followed by another, then a third more tentative attempt over 3 or 4 days. The line went dead. Maybe I'd tried too hard... Had an edge of over-keenness (which to a client can look like 'despair') crept into my voice?

Anyway, today I was in that very town... and was walking past the tourist office. One voice in my head said 'Don't bother them *again*', while the other said 'You have nothing to lose'. So I walked in, breathed deeply and asked to speak to the boss. The upshot? Walked out with a 30,000 word job. They'd just been too busy, too disorganised etc, not (as I'd thought) involved in a mass existential rejection of my very being...

The moral? Never listen to any voice in your head apart from the one that says 'Do it!'

Bouncing back, or how to turn a blow into a blessing...

Recently I had to ... ahem... 'rest' one of my freelance colleagues for a while. Just one potentially serious misunderstanding too many, (and this after a handful of gentle warnings), even though she was essentially a good egg. We had a long chat and

I explained why. Of course it was a blow, however softly it was cushioned.

Anyway, two months later we met up at a social event. We chatted and she said that after seriously questioning her career for a day or two, she'd resolved to take things in hand. She accepted that there was a certain lack of final detail in her work, and so teamed up with another translator and they now mutually review each other's translations. She told me that since then, she's never been busier and has also raised her rates...

It's not everyone who responds to feedback so courageously, and I salute her.

Recently, I once again saw the superb 'The Class' ('Entre les Murs') starring François Bégaudeau and based on the book he wrote. For those unfamiliar with the prizewinning docufilm, it's a no-holds-barred portrayal of a year in a 'difficult' school in the *banlieues* of Paris, focusing in particular on the battle of the French teacher to win over a class of kids from a whole range of cultures. Despite his best and most idealistic efforts, he's faced with a hotbed of simmering conflicts, rowdiness, insolence, ethnic tensions and mixed ability, all set in a bubbling cauldron of hormonally-charged adolescence.

There's only so much the teacher can do, even though he's clearly a competent and caring professional. There are far too many variables beyond his control. The kids' backgrounds and personal histories, their parents' sense of commitment, their family work ethic and of course their own emerging and often confused personas all thwart his vision and endeavours to educate his charges. The occasional breakthroughs where he really connects with the students are moving, but are far outweighed by the obstacles. And yet he's one of the more optimistic voices in the staffroom…

It made me realise, and not for the first time, just how few constraints there are on us as freelancers. Unlike him, we're not stuck with a fixed group of clients. We can step out of any situation, turning our backs on what we don't like. We have the right to choose who we work with. We don't have to deal with moaning colleagues all the time (we at least have the option to log out). In short, we can always say 'no'.

Rather than 'between the walls', we are in fact 'outside the walls'.

I wonder if we appreciate how free we really are?

Miranda Joubioux *I think that everyone can opt out of a situation if they want. However, it is not always as easy as it seems for anyone. It requires the ability to say 'no'. I personally had to learn this. People who have careers are bound by a lot of moulds and what is expected of them. But even they can say 'No, I'm not doing this.' Freelancers can often find themselves in a similar situation, tied up with low-paying agencies and scared to break with them, because they have to make ends meet.*

Standing Out *Sure, Miranda, we can get into a rut. But my point is that ultimately no-one is really tied up, except for in their own minds. It's unwise to make a complete break overnight: it has to be step by step, and* *over several months. But it's even more unwise to keep doing the same thing if it's making us miserable.*

Let's say you're working flat out for 3 low payers, to make ends meet. That means at the very least that you have built up a lot of experience of various text types. All it takes is half an hour to look up just two or three more promising agencies on the Blue Board and phone them, or write them an engaging message. The more targeted and personalised, the higher your chances. If just one of them takes you on, you can begin to breathe more easily and begin to plan dropping the worst of your existing three... and that's how it starts to change, bit by bit...

Miranda Joubioux *I agree with you wholeheartedly. However, fears are often irrational and feel very real to many people, even if many of us are able to go beyond them. Sometimes you need help, whether it is in the form of the written word, as here, or any other sort.*

Standing Out *I'd agree with that. Without the help and advice of a few key people in recent years, my fifth year as a translator would have been just a little better than my first year. Luckily, we're in an age where such help is highly accessible in an abundance of media.*

But it still takes the person at the centre of it all to decide to make the initial leap. What I'd love to achieve here is to help people realise it's possible. And then the hard work begins...

Anna Barbosa *I've read that the definition of insanity is always doing the same thing and expecting a different result. And I was insane for a long time... Then I realised that change had to be internal and, slowly but surely, started changing. I decided to make translation my full time job, as it was* *what I enjoyed doing the most, found a couple of small clients and then quit my teaching job. Oh, the relief of having a silent room, of not having to deal with multiple cultural backgrounds, demands and dreams, the opportunity of choosing which jobs I wanted. And I made mistakes, not a few but a lot. And I learned. And today, five years later, just like Andrew, I thank myself for the choices I've made. I really value my work and although some days are long and tough, I am a happy translator; a standing out translator, if I may say so. Oh, and I've learned the most difficult thing I ever learned: to say 'no'.*

The CV was glittering, the covering letter exemplary, and yet when I sent a (paid) test, the translation was quite simply horrendous. More wooden than Sherwood Forest.

What do you say to a translator who is very probably in the wrong job? Who would quite possibly be better off as a crane driver, window cleaner or lion tamer?

Naturally, this would never apply to any of the utterly brilliant readers of this book, but there are some people out there in dire need of career guidance...

Two translators and a horse walk into an agency.

The translators are both good, nice style, fluid texts, eye for detail. You know what I mean. Sound chaps.

The horse is just a horse. But a decent old nag too.

They sit down (not the horse), do a little test, and out pop two rather fine translations.

And when the agency owner (let's call him Joe Capitalist because he is of course in a top hat and bulging waistcoat, with dollar signs for eyes and surrounded by piles of glittering gold coins, which he counts from morning till evening) calls them one by one into his office and says 'What's your rate?', Translator 1 says '7 kopeks per word'. The dollar signs glow happily and Joe says 'Yes, ok, you're in...' Exit Translator 1, stage left.

The second translator walks in. Same question. But in reply, T2 says '10 kopeks per word'. Steam comes out of Joe's ears, the dollar signs grow just a little smaller, his pudgy little fists clench around a shiny coin. But finally, he says 'Yes, ok, you're in'.

Naturally, the translators compare findings as they go for a beer. One is slightly happier than the other, despite the fact that they both belong to the Exploited Masses.

Your task for the day. Explain what has happened and why, with references to the prevailing economic situation, human psychology and any breakfast cereal of your choice.

And when we find the answer, we can have it printed on flyers and send it to every translator in the world when they feel a rate-whinge coming on.

Meanwhile, the horse walks into the office, and (yes, you guessed it already) Joe Capitalist says 'Why the long face?

Vanessa Di Stefano *Well let's get the serious stuff out the way first. The breakfast cereal has to be All-Bran or Branflakes. Well, okay, Crunchy Nut can sneak in there too, I guess. As for the psychology and prevailing* *economic situation...well, first of all Mr Capitalist was very clever, of course, by seeing them on their own, as they then can't gang up on him and demand a fair and equal wage. Secondly, each translator could in such a situation, theoretically at least, ask for what they want, as they wouldn't have any colleagues giving them filthy looks about their price (whether too high or too low). This freedom creates a dilemma for the translator - should I go high or low? What is high or low compared to the others? And why doesn't Mr Capitalist just buy bigger clothes so that he is more comfortable? With such dilemmas you see the true character of the individual translator come out. T1 is timid, or desperate, and offers a rate they feel can't be refused. And in fact it isn't and Mr Capitalist is delighted and his eyes ping dollars. T2 is bold, or has enough work already, and so just goes for it, and asks for a high rate. And here is the moral of the story - it is accepted! And T2 would never have known that if they hadn't even tried. The horse instead is very sad as he wasn't even asked for his rate, or even to sit a test. Maybe he would have been the best of them all, but because of his appearance, he was pushed aside and ignored...*

To all freelancers who whine on about predatory agencies, evil bosses, stupid rates, impossible deadlines, unreasonable volumes of text, here's a simple dialogue which should be easy to memorise for next time. Just practise in front of a mirror and you'll soon learn your lines. However, (serious method actor that you are), do 'get into character' and work out your back-story and complex motivations...

Client: 'Can you do me [number] words at [low number] cents per word by [time]?'
Freelancer: 'No.'

Deeply unqualified though I am as a psychologist, I have been watching people for 50 years since I was born.

And so my question is this. If someone raises a problem (ooh, let's say, off the top of my head: 'evil agencies') and you point them in the direction of an answer one day, and then again, and again, and the following week they raise the same issue, plus the week after that, does this mean:

a)   the answer is wrong?
b)   the problem is imaginary?
c)   the problem is real and the answer is right, but 'hard'?
d)   the problem person actually enjoys having the problem?
e)   the problem person doesn't realise *they* are the problem?
f)   it's easier to whinge than to change?
g)   their suffering in professional life is deeply connected to their suffering in real life?
h)   whateverrrr?
i)   all of the above?
j)   none of the above?

Discuss, with reference to the film 'Groundhog Day'

Alexandra Maldwyn-Davies *I just got a call from a friend of a friend asking about getting into translation. My first piece of advice was to not listen to all the moany ponies. It's just incredible. What a waste of time. Today, I've been having a pretty bad day, but what possible good could it do me to get all down about it? I had a Trados crash at lunchtime and lost this morning's work. Annoying, but I'm over it now. I had an offer of 12,000 words for Monday. Annoying, but I just negotiated a 10 day deadline. Sorted. Don't like the emails offering 0.02 psw? Don't answer them or politely say no. Why all the clever-dick responses? Is the PM going to say 'Ha ha! That was such a cleverly worded response, I'll change the budget for this. It's now 0.12. What was I thinking?' There's plenty of work out there for everyone. I enjoy online conversations for swapping tips, sharing thoughts and experiences and having a laugh, but I can't be doing with the neighsayers and one-upmanship. If you produce good quality work, people will come back. Find the right clients. Move on. Be nice.*

Pull your socks up. Don't play with the big moany ponies.

We get the clients we deserve.

Or more subtly perhaps, we get the clients we THINK we deserve.

An afternoon thought.

Translators can manage without agencies.

But no agency can manage without translators.

So where does the power really lie?

∾

There are few things as fleeting in life as a window of opportunity.

∾

I was looking at pictures of NYC for a text I'm working on this morning, and the fire escape staircases outside so many of the old buildings seemed like a good metaphor for a career path.

(Except you're on the way up, not down, and not running away from a fire. Or at least I hope not).

In anyone's journey there are always periods of intense learning followed by periods of consolidation.

Now and again it's good to take a breather on the landing... But not for too long. Look around and enjoy the view for a while, taking in where you've got to.

And then it's time to climb again.

∾

Mega-agencies, boutique agencies, studios, freelance translators working for direct clients, freelance translators working for other freelance translators, freelance translators working for agencies...

I think we all end up precisely where we should be along the food chain at any given point, though this naturally grows and shifts over time.

59

In other words, we get *exactly* the conditions we deserve. No more, no less.

And if we're not happy, it's a signal that we need to step up and change something.

Starting with ourselves.

∾

Many freelance translators spend an inordinate amount of time attempting to adjust the world around them in line with their expectations.

That's broadly a good thing... I do believe that we create our own reality much of the time.

But sometimes, it's also good to adjust our expectations and keep them in check.

And especially to avoid comparing with what others say they are doing/earning (irrespective of whether it's true or not).

Knowing where we're at right now and where we can reasonably get to next is wiser than setting a goal far in the distance, constantly failing to match up to it and then feeling depressed.

Small steps and realistic goals generate more achievement and more confidence...

We build our worlds piece by piece.

Sara Freitas *I mostly agree. I do think having a long-term goal is important as a framework for the smaller everyday 'where I am right now' goals. As business owners an annual income goal is key. As freelancers defining* *that ideal type of client or project is also important... I say set a five-year plan and check in with yourself on a regular basis.*

Peter Bowen *This has been puzzling me for a while. I hope they also adjust themselves to the world around them in line with the expectations of others. This is called socialisation......! Disconnecting from the world beyond your office walls is not a good thing and goals and targets and achievements are only relevant in terms of the wider world. The key is to find the balance between you and it. I must confess to frequent falls into the canyon.*

In my first three years I gained a handful of important direct clients... perhaps a little prematurely... one or two were too demanding for my skills and experience at the time, and though I delivered my best shot with every translation, a couple of them faded away over the years.

So when this week I was about to embark on my annual summer search for new clients, I discussed this with Brigitte.

She said 'Dig out those old clients, try them again!'

'Nah!' quoth I. 'No point, in translation once you've lost a client, you can never go back, cap in hand.'

As you can see, it wasn't my most upbeat moment... (it happens, even to me).

'Rubbish!' rejoined the fair Brigitte. 'You've got nothing to lose. Stop being such a bloody milksop.'

(I'm translating liberally from the French, you understand). One such client was a major international organisation which outsources some of its immense body of translation work. So, suppressing my disbelief, I fired off an email in a bottle saying that my website had changed, that I had more experience, and that I'd just love to work with them again.

Less than 24 hours later, 14,000 words hit my inbox. The moral of this story?

a) Never give up.
b) Everything changes.
c) Nothing happens unless you make it happen.
d) Always listen to Brigitte.

Mary Kyr *Everything changes, that's so true! We have to continuously evolve and adapt if we want to stay afloat.*

Paula Castelão *The moral of this story? 'Behind every great (male) translator...'*

It's always good to play a little ping-pong with agencies...

Yesterday one of them contacted me for the first time in ages. Over a year in fact.

No I tell a lie, they wrote to me last week, but a general newsletter. Whereupon your humble correspondent penned a very polite letter back saying 'It's been a long time since I translated for you. Perhaps you should remove me from your mailing list. Or better still, send me some work.'

They had been good payers and fun to deal with and I'd never quite worked out at what point we'd drifted apart. Anyway, I'd consigned the experience to the learning drawer and pretty much forgotten about them. Even after the newsletter exchange I didn't really expect much to transpire.

So when I heard from them in the afternoon, I was naturally quite pleased…

However, when I opened the email and saw the task, a few seeds of doubt were sown: it was the transcription and then translation of a French audio file. Said seeds grew into alarm-flowers when I opened the file and it seemed to have been recorded using an empty beer can and a piece of string inside a shoebox at the bottom of the ocean a gazillion miles from where the speaker was talking. Large parts of it were completely inaudible.

So I simply sent it back and said 'Sorry, chaps, it's impossible. Life's too short.' (Or words to that effect).

They then asked me if I could transcribe just the audible bits. Which was a bit absurd as that was about 50% of the text. Rather than saying no twice in a row, I then suggested to them they should contact a French native speaker for the transcription and use me for the translation part?

Which is exactly what they ended up doing. So now everyone's happy.

Looking back, it's clear that at three points in the story, I exercised a bit of power, flexed a little muscle, and acted as a partner in dialogue, not as a subordinate. Which is how I see the optimal translator-agency relationship working.

Just a reminder that between a subservient 'yes' and a belligerent 'no' there are 50 shades of 'maybe'.

Gill McKay *Absolutely, agency and translator should be a team who work together to give the customer the best possible result.*

Deborah DC *Agree. I regularly lob the ball back over the net, as I put it - in NL>EN the game is tennis, not ping-pong - and it often leads to a good outcome. And even when it doesn't, you've shown some flexibility but with the ability to be firm, which sets the right tone for the future anyhow.*

Ellen Yutzy Glebe *I know you have a long list, but have you considered '50 Shades of Maybe' as a possible title for a future book?*

Peter Bowen *Yes, important to remember you and they are equals. I received a 'Dear Linguist' email today from an agency PM with whom I had previously corresponded, only to finish with despair on my part at their rate. I was on the point of replying with 'Dear Agency' but thought better of it. The revenge would have been sweet, but there is little point is expending too much choler on someone at the other end of an email line, and you never know where a measured response might lead.... maybe I will be amazed...*

Recently another agency contacted me based on the ITI directory, right out of the blue.

Their opening gambit was quite laconic, along the lines of

'We found you in the ITI listing, can you do a translation for us?'

No mention on the Blue Board, but a professional-looking website.

Let's take a chance. There is, after all, no such thing as a coincidence.

My reply: 'Sure, looks doable, but I prefer to have a conversation with all new clients before undertaking a first job, so can you give me a call?'

Half an hour later they called, and I realised that by some subtle alchemy, it was in fact me who was interviewing them.

Isn't that how it should be with agencies? Instead of kowtowing and falling over with gratitude each time you get an approach, you see it as a partnership of equals. They provide the clients, you provide the service.

It should come across in your voice, in the very way you speak. Polite, enthusiastic and self-confident.

But it's not enough just to talk the talk. You have to believe it. And there's the real challenge.

.

4 THE PERFECT LIKENESS

A sculptor was once asked how he could carve such a magnificent likeness of his own head out of a block of marble. His reply? 'I simply remove that which isn't me.'

I first started as a full-time translator five years ago. Like just about everyone, I accepted whatever work came my way from the various agencies who deigned to take me on. Council meeting minutes, perfume descriptions, environmental awareness leaflets and restaurant menus.

True, I enjoyed some translations more than others, either for the fascination of their content or the flow of their prose, but I simply saw such highs and lows as a normal part of the job. Still, I was mildly troubled by the fact that I felt so alive when translating the history of a cathedral and quite so beset by a sense of gloom when wading through pages of what Mr X said to Ms Y at Meeting Z.

This was compounded of course by the commonly held belief that surely a good translator should be able to turn even plodding prose into gold?

Now I know better. It is of course entirely possible to weave golden thread out of council minutes, *but it helps a great deal if such documents light your fire* – if the cut and thrust of dialogue and policy are what get you springing out of bed in the morning, punching the air.

There are translators like that, just as there are those who are impassioned by ball bearings, captivated by nuclear power, scintillated by mediaeval art or riveted by financial analyses.

Each of us has a unique contribution to make to the world of translation. But only if we first reflect on who we are and what inspires us, and honour that.

It was Edison who said that genius is 1% inspiration, 99% perspiration. But like all clichés, it's only partly true. Have you ever noticed that on the days you are 99% inspired, you forget all about perspiration? How when you are in 'the zone', or in 'flow', or 'the element', your mind and body sing with the translation you are producing?

The day I learnt to follow my intuition in terms of choices was the day I freed myself from the shackles of duty, and the hard labour of working on texts I did not love. The doleful execution of activities that failed to make my brain fizzle and my limbs tingle was something I left behind in the faded classrooms of my schooldays. Life's too short for that.

It was also the day I realised I would never be able to translate chemistry, architecture or legal texts, whereas on the contrary, history, religion, art and culture, and especially travel topics had me skipping to my computer.

The day I specialised, I did so not because every blog, book and website in the world told me to do so, or even because it would increase my profitability in a certain sector, but because I finally understood it was my perfect right as a freelancer to do what I love and to love what I do.

My aim ever since I understood that truth has been to cultivate it further by chipping away at the vast monolithic block that is the world of translation until I reveal my own likeness.

It's an option that's open to everyone.

Take a hefty swing at things that really turn you off, as I did the first time I ever sat in front of a 3,000 word text on the nuclear industry. Pick up a finer chisel as you hone in closer on the form you want. Decide on history, for example, but perhaps not the history of science. Embrace the fine arts museums but subtly chip away the industrial museums.

Likewise with your clients. Over time, lop off those whose methods or rates do not suit your temperament, whose working practices are too hurried or not quality-conscious enough for you. Whittle away until you are left with the ideal clients, whether agencies or direct, with whom you find it easy and a joy to work.

And then carve away at how you spend your time. Outsource your accounts, fill more time with writing, or take on more proofreading and editing and delegate out your website design.

What should emerge is a working life that resembles you and your deepest motivations in every way – a perfect likeness of you. And as you change over the years, make further modifications to your creation. It's a work in progress.

So if you want 99% inspiration, just copy the sculptor. And remove all that isn't you.

First published on the ITI Pillar Box Blog[5]

A freelancer facing the world of translation immediately encounters a dizzying array of possibilities: texts on every subject under the sun, clients ranging from the most corporate multi-language vendor to the smallest boutique agency, and direct clients from the small start-up round the corner to a blue-chip financial company, city museum or airline. Your rates, and therefore income, can also vary hugely from barely getting by to enjoying a prosperous lifestyle. There are short creative texts and major projects requiring months of work, solo jobs and team efforts, urgent requests and novels which can drift over months.

How to cut a swathe through the jungle? As you progress, machete in hand, hot, bothered and occasionally lost, you'll notice that in every tree there is a wise animal giving you advice: chattering monkeys, colourful parrots, buzzing insects and hissing snakes. The thing is, while their brilliant ideas and tips provide useful standards against which to weigh up your judgement and experience, none of them is you. None of them has your unique profile, experience, family and financial situation, values, needs, goals or passions.

So listen by all means. But remember to forge your own path.

5 http://www.iti.org.uk/news-media-industry-jobs/the-pillar- box/ list-by-date/613-the-perfect-likeness

Wonderful quote from Daniel Pink, the sociologist, about being freelance and working alone: 'The worst part [...] is that you have to work twenty-four hours a day. The best part is that you get to choose which twenty-four'.

How to enjoy your job 99% of the time...

A while back I got a text about irrigation tubes. Now I don't know about you, but I'm not a huge tubophile (art, tourism, film festivals, history and international politics are much more my thing), and so by the time I got to the end of the first sentence, I was already contemplating the meaninglessness of my existence. No way was I going to devote two days of my life to a bit of metal in a field.

But a client is a client. I put an ad on ProZ and lo and behold, got a man who spent his life dreaming about tubes (yes, people like that exist). That day I learnt something important: there is no subject on earth that won't inspire *somebody*.

So if you get a text which doesn't make you spring out of bed in the morning, don't turn it down (bad business sense), but why not take it and outsource it to someone who *will* love it. That's one way to get to love your job almost all the time. Keep what inspires you and delegate the rest.

About 2 years ago, I visited a big agency I've been with for ages and the head honcho intimated to me that there was a project manager's job going.

Sweeping his hand across the office, he seemed to be saying: 'All this could be yours, my son.' I looked (an expression of polite interest masking my sinking sense of *Weltschmerz*) from grey cubicle to grey cubicle in the pallid light of the capital city, took in the low buzz of constant chatter on phones against a background of music-less silence, the endless clatter of fingers on keyboards, the clicking of pens...and thought of my home office, my favourite music, the view of trees and fields, the fact that I don't have to say 'Good morning' in a cheerful tone to 50 people every day... and the right to wear my Snoopy pyjamas while I work (OK I made that bit up).

Not to mention the fact that I work when I want, for whom I want and don't need a signature in triplicate if I want to buy a new printer.

Not for the first time, but very much *sotto voce*, I said to myself: 'Thank God I was born a freelancer.'

Volker Freitag *You may choose to work in-house to get started and gain some experience (although it is usually quite hard to find an in-house position if you don't already have a lot of experience). Once you are experienced enough and know how much you could make as a freelancer, it is odd that you should choose to stay on.*

Translated letter sent this morning to an (ex-?)prospect. Sometimes it just feels good to say these things... (and get in there first!)

Dear XXX

Many thanks for taking the time to meet me yesterday afternoon. However, my initial impression is that Morristraduction will be unable to work with you in this instance. In our discussions you made it clear that your primary criterion in selecting a translation partner was price. (This might explain, incidentally, why out of 8 public signs in English in your office, 6 contained spelling or grammar mistakes). While our prices are competitive, our main focus is and must remain on excellence.

I wish you luck in your search for a more suitable partner. Our door is open should your priorities change.

Best wishes
Andrew Morris

Here's another formula I've been working on. For the mathematically uninitiated amongst us, it boils down to this: at the beginning of the year I put my (word) rate up for my oldest and best-paying agency client. Half-expecting, despite myself, to receive slightly less work, and take that in my stride.

The result? They've sent me twice as much work since. Perhaps there's a simple moral in there... the more you value yourself, the more others simply have little choice but to follow suit...

Once upon a time there was a frog in a forest, sitting on a lily pond. Butterflies danced through the air, dragonflies whizzed by in a flash of blue. The frog hadn't worked for a while, and began to feel sorry for himself. Then out of the corner of his eye, he saw a princess on the bank. She said 'I can kiss you and turn you into a prince, but first you'll have to do me 3,000 words at your 'best rate' and by yesterday evening, please.'

The frog hummed and hawed... this would pay the rent on the lily pad for a while and he'd always wanted to wear a crown... but then he came to his senses and said 'I'd rather remain a freelance frog than accept those conditions, so bugger off.'

The princess stormed off, swearing in a way that was most unlike a princess. Meanwhile, on other lily pads, frogs who had accepted the princess's earlier promises muttered darkly about imported tadpoles from China and India and how the whole pond was being threatened by machine lilies.

Not long after, the frog, in top hat and tails, stood in front of his newly painted 'Frog Studio', greeting his direct clients with champagne, just like a prince would.

And the moral of this tale is... well you'll just have to work that out for yourselves.

Potential client contacted me with quite an interesting culture piece yesterday. Sent a reply. He rang, and we chatted for about 30 minutes. Because that's what you do with a new client, especially if there's a juicy text ahead...

I did a free short test, whereupon he phoned me. Another 20 minutes. Because that's what you do etc etc...

And I even made a couple of adjustments to his test. Because etc etc.

But when he phoned a third time to discuss the position of a preposition, I began to realise there is such a thing as the Client from Hell.

Time to bail out or double my price...

Funny thing is, every marketing or 'tips-for-translators site' I ever came across said 'Do a blog'.

I looked from right to left, and beheld a whole bunch of very interesting blogs in pretty colours. Some were serious, some light-hearted, some for translators, some for clients.

'Good grief,' I said to myself, 'Looks like an awful lot of hard work.'

But try as I might, for me it just wouldn't come.

And then one day, just when I wasn't looking, it bubbled up. And out. It demanded to be written, it nipped my ankles, until I let it off the leash.

And I learnt a key lesson. Whatever you do has to come from within. Because when it comes from inside, it's true.

Marie Jackson *Absolutely true! I launched my blog in January... but it took a long time for me to come around to the idea. I just didn't feel I had much to say! Then, one day, I found I had lots to say but nowhere to say it. If your heart isn't in it then you may as well spend your precious time doing things in which you are fully present.*

Ever get the impression your life is ruled by deadlines? After initial discussions with my web designer over the new angle I wanted for my forthcoming site (version 3!), the kind of audience I was now targeting, and the overall 'feel' he said, brightly, 'Ok, just give me a couple of weeks and I'll come up with something.'

Now as he's a creative chap, I'm very happy to do that... Maybe I'll even adopt that line with my clients.

'Just love your text... let me spend some time on it and I'll get back to you when I'm ready, ok?'

Think it'll work?

One or two of my favourite agencies are very good about sending back texts I've particularly liked working on. I don't ask every time, but it's a naughty pleasure I indulge in once in a while.

At this point the art of the facepalm becomes a very important skill to master.

For neophytes, these are the steps:

1.   Open up your original text and the proofread version side by side.
2.   Note with pleasure that most of the text has remained unchanged.
3.   Zoom in like a hornet on the one word where (of course) the agency, with fresh eyes, has come up with a witty, piquant and very pertinent replacement for the word you already thought was the bee's knees.
4.   Remove glasses (crucial)
5.   Open your hand and slap hard on your forehead.
6.   Resume text and return to point 2.

Note for proud translators: there is a lesser-known variation on the game where you feel your original word was in fact better and want to slap the proofreader's forehead rather than your own.

Note for sado-masochists: too much of this can damage your health.

I wonder if translators develop flatter foreheads over the years?

The single best piece of advice anyone ever offered me since I started out in translation was this:

Don't compare yourself to anyone else. Ever. It's easy to say, not always easy to achieve. Watch, learn, even emulate, but never compare.

If you won your country's national lottery and became a millionaire overnight, would you stop translating?

For a day? For a week? For a year? Forever?

Allison Wright *No.*

Ode Laforge *As I think I would spend my time travelling to foreign countries ... translating would become even more part of my life, to continue to communicate with people of different cultures!*

If you were offered a fully equipped office anywhere in the world for a month, with perfect communication lines to the outside world (and guaranteed top quality coffee of course), where would you choose?

a) a beach hut overlooking the ocean?
b) a luxury pad overlooking Central Park?
c) a hut up a mountain?
d) a hut in the middle of a deep forest?
e) a loft in Paris? London? Barcelona?
f) any other idea of your choosing

Why? What do you think your choice says about you? And what element might it inject into your life that you'd like to see more of?

Let your imagination out to play!

Rebecca Darby Sims *I'd pick each one in turn. Flats in Berlin, Hamburg and various Scandinavian places would also feature, not forgetting a country pile somewhere in the south of France. Possibly Italy and/or Spain as well. What about Melbourne, preferably near the Bay? Thailand, Japan, Singapore, Brazil, Ecuador, Chile, the list goes on...*

About three years ago a direct client from the academic sector sent me a text about the environment.

It was a subject that I could have tackled at a push, with a fair amount of research, but when I opened the text up, there was just something about it that didn't grab me.

Did I really want to spend three days in this marshy world? Sure, I could do with the money, but there again that nagging feeling wouldn't go away...

I decided to outsource it (my website clearly stated that I worked with a team) and soon found a competent professional on ProZ. They translated it so well that the client began to recommend our services to other colleagues in different fields, and since then I would say about 20 new clients have grown out of that single initial decision.

There are two lessons here: one, the obvious one, is that you need to make sure the quality is as good as it can possibly be at all times.

But two is that I'm pretty sure that if I'd translated it myself, ignoring that insistent inner voice, the outcome would have been satisfactory, but perhaps little more.

How often do we ignore our intuitions? In my life as a translator, every time I've ignored them it's led to a setback, and a lesson learned.

Which is good of course. It all feeds in to your professional development.

But when you tune in and listen to what the deepest part of your mind is trying to tell you in the first place, it's so much better.

Mary Kyr *We should always be mindful of our instincts and look out for the signs. I have recently been thinking about pursuing a career as an interpreter and I started looking for seminars, workshops or private schools, both* *in Greece and in the UK. A few weeks ago one of my oldest clients called me and asked me to interpret for him in a business meeting, although he knows very well that I'm a translator. I wanted to help him so I escorted him to the meeting and ended up doing consecutive interpretation for 3 hours straight. I felt so alive! It was an exhilarating experience, the client was very happy with my services and the company he had the meeting with asked me to interpret for them once more the day before yesterday! So clearly the universe told me that this is the right way to go.*

I took a quick online tour round the word 'workaholic' this fine Easter Monday morning.

Funny thing is, I never see myself as a workaholic in the slightest...

Now you're just going to say I'm in denial. But no, I'm just someone who enjoys what he does, and doesn't draw a strong line between time on and time off.

One article I saw, by the gloriously named Dr Brad Klontz, suggested we all take the rocking chair test.

'Picture yourself at retirement age sitting on your front porch rocking in your chair. Looking back on your life, where do you wish you had spent more time? At the office? On the golf course? On vacation with your family?'

But better still, why wait till then? I ask myself just about each day (each moment?) what I want to be doing.

And the answer is pretty much always 'this'.

Gill McKay *We all find our own balance, but the rocking chair test is definitely the key. I'm happy to be working today while it's grey outside. It means I can take a few extra hours off later in the week when the sun is shining and I feel more in need of a break - and somehow it's always more fun when you know everyone else is stuck in the office!*

A translator contacts me for a coaching session, saying she's been working on what really drives her as a translator and getting ideas together for a website but somehow can't break through. Her head is spinning, she's confused.

I ask her to send me something about her specialisms, and a little of her backstory as a translator, including specifically what she loves about language and the job.

She writes in her specialisms that she wants to focus on economics, finance and pharmaceuticals, which is where she has some experience. She's done that before. It's what she knows.

Fair enough.

She then appends a four page document which is absolutely full of her enthusiasm for English-speaking culture, gardening, cookery, history and poetry. Describing the latter, she talks of how she responds with her mind and body ('It sends shivers down my spine').

Nowhere does she mention scientific journals, finance reviews, economics documentaries or anything of the sort.

When I tentatively suggest during her session that perhaps the confusion comes from the disconnect between the 'safe' and 'secure' specialisms she feels she 'ought' to be doing (her mind speaking) and the things that really inspire her (her heart speaking), she is amazed.

'I never thought of it like that before.'

We can often convince ourselves of something using clever arguments. And end up doing what we feel we should be doing rather than what we really want to do.

In any debate between mind and heart, it's always the heart that wins out in the end.

If we listen, that is...

Sometimes your words come back to haunt you.

Yesterday I was trying to outsource an admittedly not very inspiring text, when my colleague pointed out that it wouldn't make her spring out of bed in the morning and actually had the temerity to cite my own article about the sculptor in her defence.

She's right of course. Bugger!

An agency writes to me with a very interesting copywriting offer. Tourism, and in a place I know well.

It's one of my very first real breaks in copywriting. But the offer is half what I'd normally expect for the amount of time involved.

One part of me based somewhere in my head wants to leap up and down, grasp the opportunity.

Another more intuitive part says 'You know your price. If you're not 100% convinced, don't do it.'

I listen to the second part and send off a polite 'Thanks but no thanks.'

Why? Because I simply know that the space left will be filled by something better round the corner. And sometimes it's good to clear the way...

Don't ask me how I know. I just do.

.

Nelia Fahloun *I did something similar this week (turning down work at a low rate), with absolutely no idea if other work would arrive. But it did: better paid and more interesting!*

My entire week thus far has been devoted to translations in the following areas:

- Abstract art and Expressionism
- Holistic approaches to health
- Christmas tourism in Germany
- The history of a well-known Swiss drink
- Avignon in the 14th century
- The art market in Africa and the Middle East

- Skiing in Morocco (I kid you not)

Which is more or less exactly what I want to be working on. Getting the hang of this sculpting thing.

(PS Coming up with the metaphor is the easy part. You then have to go out and do it).

5 THE ENTREPRENEUR'S APPRENTICE

Small is beautiful

If you spend an hour on New York's legendary Times Square, and observe what people consume, you'll be amazed. You'll see giants drinking Coke from buckets, others holding burgers the size of frisbees, while yet others ravage boxfuls of donuts (sic), as well as downing milkshakes, chomping on snacks and wolfing down bars of chocolate as big as chessboards.

It's junk food paradise, or hell, depending on your point of view.

And if you magically levitate up over the skyscrapers and peruse the city, state and even the entire country beyond, you will swiftly become aware of the industrialisation and mechanisation of food production. Not to mention the deafening clamour of the agribusiness conglomerates, drowning out the voice of healthy eating.

However, if you return to earth, go underground, and emerge after a clattering subway ride into the leafy, spacious streets of Greenwich Village, you'll be immediately struck by the contrast. Human-sized houses, pavement cafés and farmers' markets. That's more like it. You might even, on a good day, see some people eating vegetables.

Just a hop further into Chelsea will bring you to the doors of the Blossom Restaurant, with its burnished wood interior, elegant pictures on the walls and soft lighting. The menu is reassuringly expensive. The wine, as ever in the States, is rather more unnervingly expensive – a single glass costing as much as a family meal in a fast food restaurant.

But hey, you only live once.

Looking around at the room, which is full to capacity, you might be forgiven for wondering how a restaurant which is not only organic and vegetarian, but pricey and classy to boot, could hold its own in a city so apparently devoted to ingesting garbage. The food turns out to be excellent, and as you leave you note the queue of around 40 people lining up on the off chance a table might become free.

Business is obviously booming at the Blossom.

Your mind wanders to some of the finest restaurants you've been to, in your own home town and when travelling. You've read the welter of bad news about the food industry, the explosion of allergies, the mechanisation and industrialisation and the dominance of the entire world food sector by giant corporations unaffected by any principle other than that of profit. But you also know from your own experience of restaurant after bistro after café opening up in every village, town and city in the world and making a success of it.

Slowly, a parallel begins to form in your mind's eye with the world of translation. There too, you don't have to look far to pick up on dire warnings of mechanisation and industrialisation. The names of the mega-corporates are on many lips. Everyone knows – or claims to know – who the bad guys are. Prices are being driven down, just as they are for farmers throughout the world. Examples of translation whose quality is no better than that of a triple decker with fries are routinely trotted out. A climate of unease lingers like the smell of frying fat in the air. Here too, allergies fester.

And yet, the Blossom example has something to tell us as translators. Sure, things can look pretty grim if you see yourself as competing against the behemoths. How can you possibly mobilise the same resources and produce the same quantity as them? But here's the thing. They aren't the competition. They're not even on your planet.

When they started out, the owners of Blossom clearly decided they wanted to specialise in a certain sector. They opted to focus on absolute quality, target a highly select, minority niche market and charge prices consistent with the excellence of their cuisine. They had the skills of course, and no doubt had learned the ropes through hard-won experience. But when the time was right they launched. And soon began to soar.

Presumably they had their views on the fast food chains, and no doubt they secretly disapproved. But they also understood the glorious irrelevance to their own daily lives. They didn't need 82 million customers per day, they needed between sixty and a hundred.

You need six to ten.

And that's per week, if not per month.

On the first day of their launch, they must have been apprehensive about what lay ahead. But they rose to the challenge and believed in the goal they had set themselves, and in just a few years were being showered with five-star write-ups on every restaurant review site in the world.

So why not follow their example? Rather than focusing on the threats around every corner, pursue your own niche market with equal determination, enthusiasm and an incessant attention to the quality of what you do.

And before too long, you too might find there are people queuing outside the door.

First published in the ITI Bulletin

Here's a thought. What if low rates actually flowed towards those who don't believe in themselves enough? If someone offers me a rate I don't like, I exercise my right as a freelancer to tell them to bugger off. I'd rather go hungry than sell myself cheap. I did that in my first ever week on ProZ and then never again. And the irony is, I never got hungry...

One of my professional heroes Walt Kania of www. thefreelancery.com advocates doubling your rates and seeing what happens. OK, that may be a little far fetched... But having said that, yesterday a regular client contacted me to check about 6 sentences. I said 'Sure, but it'll cost you half an hour of my time,' (and decided on the spot that my hourly rate was going to increase by 25%). He didn't bat an eyelid. If you don't ask, you don't get.

Maybe rather than expecting big agencies to get all generous, individual translators should stand up for themselves more. Or seek out smaller agencies. In my capacity as one of the latter, I respect those translators who say 'I'm putting my rate up'.

As long as they don't say it once a day.

No logo, wrote the great Naomi Klein. But personally, I had one before I even began translating my first word.

I've always thought of presentation, the shop window effect, etc etc, as crucial. We may disparage 'image' (and rightly so if the reality doesn't back it up) but nevertheless in the 21st century, image counts, and a logo (plus website) is an easy and effective way to stand out from the crowd. So, to logo or not to logo? Discuss.

In the course of a bid to put together a team for an important but small project, I asked two contacts in different agencies, both of whom I've known for years, for recommendations for a certain language pair. Both were tight-lipped and said either I could hand over the project or sorry, they couldn't help.

As a boutique agency, when people ask me for recommendations, I am *delighted* to pass on good names. Done it loads of times. What is there to lose? If my best colleagues are a) more active and b) less dependent on me, it's win-win. (Of course if they disappear then it's my problem, but that seems unlikely as I still believe in the old values of loyalty and team spirit).

We all know how difficult it is for translators to get new clients, and I firmly believe in giving good people a leg-up. Am I just a naive simpleton? (Don't answer that…)

Received this morning: 'Dear Sir, Thank you for your wonderful response of our 'September '13 Price List'. We are an ISO 9001-2008 Certified Company and Ansh Laureate. We present to you the WORLD'S LARGEST PRICE LIST (only for Translation Companies) with more than 1200 languages pairs on offer along with 300 Transcription and some Subtitling offers.

We are trusted for our services by more than 300 Translation Agencies for their complete/ occasional needs of regular/ difficult/ odd/ rare language translation projects. Do keep our price list handy to refer at such times when your regular translator is busy, or if the language pair is rare/ unavailable. You may also offer us your strong language pairs and we will add them to our strength.

Our rates are good and we don't deal with direct clients ensuring that your business is cost effective, simple and our offer does not disturb your offered market rates.

Wishing you your best years ahead. Affectionately, XXXXXXXX'

Between the 'response of', the 'languages pairs', the 'regular translator' (just the one), and the non-disturbing offer, I'm wondering whether to write back and offer them MY proofreading services. Although I'm not sure I can do that in 1,200 languages...

Affectionately of course.

By the way, the XXXXs are to mask the writer's name and are not meant to represent kisses...

And yes, the best years are ahead of us all...

There's been plenty of debate around image versus content. Of course a mediocre translator won't go far, even if they employ a full-time Madison Avenue image consultant... but that doesn't mean image is unimportant.

A new translator contacted me recently. Promising website, very good style. I then offered him his first text, during a Skype IM chat. 'Sure,' he answered. 'Got time before going out to get drunk tonight'. Innocuous enough, but possibly a case of too much information?

As it happened, that text was recalled immediately by the client and he wasn't available the next day. But when, a week later, I offered another, he said 'Can't, mate (sic). Wife's away and the kids are playing hell.'

By now two tiny alarm bells are ringing. While other people's personal life is none of my concern, I might legitimately feel slightly unnerved by the mild impression of chaos... Will my text be delivered on time? Will it have wine stains on it?

As it happened, I persevered, as my initial instinct was that he was good. And sure enough, the third time we ended up with a very fine translationcreationadaptation indeed.

But it almost didn't happen. While the pally tone of instant messaging and Facebook itself can blur the boundaries between pro and personal, for my part, at least, I try to keep the two as separate as possible, in all my communications, even the (apparently) ephemeral ones. Be friendly, be funny, but don't be a loser.

Social media are great, but they also, like it or not, act as a permanent showcase for your 'brand'. As does just about everything you say in corresponding with a relatively unknown provider of work.

So I would NEVER, for example, publicise the fact that I dress up as a banana in my spare time and sing Abba songs while eating 100 jelly babies for breakfast.

Oops...

As usual, I finished my email with 'And I hope you were satisfied with our translation and our service.' Sent it off with a flourish. Another job done. Patted myself on the back.

15 minutes later, a reply. 'Actually there was one rather elementary mistake.'

At this point, without even reading on, those little adrenalin guys in my body start popping, jiving, even twerking, running everywhere. Nuclear sirens sound, it's red alert in there. Meanwhile, my brain leaps into punctuation-free mode:

'Oh my god which of my translators did this how did I miss it in proofreading what would they say on the forum perhaps I should try an alternative career as a musician my translation days are over'

You know how it goes. And all in about 1.5 seconds. But then I read a little further, to see that the client has accused us of turning a singular subject plural, and using 'they' when it should have been 'he'. As in, 'When the visitor to the museum arrives, the first thing they see is the shop.'

Aaaah! Deep breath, before writing: 'Thank you for your comments. We do take all feedback very seriously, but perhaps you are unaware that in modern English...(followed by polite explanation).'

2 minutes later, another reply from the client. 'I do apologise. Please excuse my ignorance.' Whereupon Morristraduction of course becomes supremely gracious and magnanimous in victory...

Lesson: ALWAYS ask for feedback. It may conceal an opportunity to educate and win back a client who might even have disappeared for good based on a misapprehension. And even if negative comments are justified, they contain a signal that something in your quality process needs a tweak. And as such, they're potentially more valuable than a happy customer who just says 'We were pleased.'

Anyway, I think I can put off that alternative career for another day...

A day in the life of a solopreneur part 23.

Got up at 5 am to beat the traffic to meet a client who has already awarded me the contract, but wanted to put a face to a name. Drove a total of 2.5 hours there and back (in the driving rain!) for a 45 minute chat.

Now if I was a bean counter I would look at my morning and calculate:

Working hours lost, cost of petrol (plus tolls), wear and tear on tyres, plus my poor body, lost sleep for my darling partner, and finally cost of horrible coffee in a service station whose unutterable bleakness made Edward Hopper look like Alice in Wonderland.

But as your (enter religious book of choice) would no doubt say, man (and woman) does not live by beans alone.

What did I get in return? A handshake, a smile, a nice chat, some compliments on my French accent (priceless) and (just possibly) the beginning of a beautiful client friendship.

Building a business is about more than just beans. Into the equation you also have to enter energy, connection (mental and physical), hope, the thrill of watching things grow, and three teaspoonfuls of optimism.

And then it all balances out.

Recipe for agency rate-raising
Cooking time: 2 days
Serves: 1, but potentially many more. Success rate: around 80%

1. Take one client and place in a large mixing bowl. Pour in your existing happy relationship, two pinches of hope and about a bucket of confidence. Stir well.

2. Wait until you're feeling very upbeat (crucial) and send off a letter saying 'I really enjoy working with you but have so much on that I can't possibly take on work at x any more. My rate will now be y. But of course, in return you'll have the usual fast replies, the quality, the coruscating wit and the friendly attitude. I really hope we can continue working together.'

3. Count to three and send. Leave to cool for 24 hours.

4. Read the reply. 'We understand your position but are rather surprised as the trend is for rates to be dropping.'

5. Add another half a cup of chutzpah. Say brightly: 'Ah, but I never follow trends.'

6. Await the next day, and note that a new text arrives.
7. Take three breaths. Send a message saying 'So we're agreed on the rate?'
8. Receive message saying 'Yes, but not one single typo!'
9. Laugh it off. 'Yessir! Understood!'
10. Wait till evening. Open bottle of wine to taste...

I've begun asking clients for recommendations to put in a lovely long list on my website. They all know upfront where it's going, because I ask them to go and look at the existing comments first. And they've more or less all complied.

It's certainly better than just a list of clients, and when you have quite a few, it makes a powerful case for using your services.

We clearly believe what other people say more than we believe the claims made by service providers themselves... Just think of all the decisions you've made based on Tripadvisor or Amazon reviews (the decent ones, not the ones written by people who are obviously deranged).

So why not start collecting today?

Today I'm translating the website of a translation agency I occasionally work for. And one I like.

Are they competition for me? Technically, perhaps, (same country) but I honestly couldn't care less. I am so very, very bored with reading about competition. I want this to be the best translation I can possibly produce. I want them to do well. Why? Because there can never be too much quality around.

And because those are the standards I'd want for myself if I were a client.

Despite the fact that however good the work I produce may aspire to be, it'll never be as good as the perfectionist in my brain wants it to be.

A simple thought... we sometimes forget how much energy and emotion our clients invest in texts, even if they may seem less than inspiring to us. A price list, a set of terms and conditions, instructions for 'How to get here'.

At the moment I'm having my website redesigned. Again. And realising in the process how every tiny last detail means something to me, and kind of taking for granted that the creative, gifted, expensive (and patient) web designer is with me every step of the way...

Note to self: from now on treat every single project as if it was actually my own, rather than the client's...

Of open doors and seizing the day, part 347.

At a recent three-day workshop, we were invited to select one or two of our best translations for a display table, along with our business cards.

There were 70 people on the course (40 EN>FR and 30 FR>EN). The table is big. Two people displayed their work.

I was one of them.

I also laid out 30 business cards. There were 5 left at the end.

As for the others, who knows? Perhaps they were over-flowing with clients? Or maybe reluctant to put themselves forward? Or possibly afraid of the judgement of others?

My take is this. If 20 people read my translation and 19 don't like it, but one does, (and somehow something comes of it) it's one more than if no-one reads my translation.

That's just math(s).

Miranda Joubioux *There is none so critical as another translator. Having had my work completely rewritten once by another translator, who didn't particularly improve it I might say, I can understand this apprehension. Many of us are self-critical and lack confidence. I am not at all surprised.*

Standing Out *I wouldn't say I'm always brimming with confidence about my translations either. But in this case, there is nothing to lose... If they criticise me behind my back, I don't care. If to my face, I'd say 'Show me yours' And if theirs is better than mine, bingo, free training!!*

On fear and trembling...

A colleague suggested recently that it was not a good idea to give too much away on a Facebook page, lest readers secretly hunt out my clients. 'No-one is irreplaceable,' they said, reasonably enough. Now while I'm hardly going to post the telephone numbers, budgets and inside leg measurements of my various contacts here, I do wonder about this culture of fear.

When you develop a direct client base, treat them well, get to know them personally, and do your best to deliver good service, then it's highly unlikely they will switch to someone else. Of course, a new manager may arrive, with an address book of their own. Your contact may move on. But even then, in most cases, people want an easy life. They don't want to begin the search all over again...

Your friendly client might also of course fall in love with a tall, dark and handsome translator. But there are relatively few male translators, so there's hope.

And I am fairly convinced that rare is the client who will switch based on price alone, without at least trying to negotiate with you.

I am also reasonably confident that values such as loyalty and trust, (which were incidentally the very backbone of my father's small town family business, which he inherited from *his* father) still count for something.

And even if one day, someone did pinch 1, 2, or 3 of my clients, well so what? Nothing is permanent. I'd just go out and find some more...

Because the one great and incontrovertible benefit of having built a business from scratch, is that you know you can always do it all over again.

Yesterday I did my first ever 4-language project.

Ok, ok so it was only an education certificate, but it *did* go into EN, DE, IT and ES.

The downside: maybe I have to change my plans for a funky translation studio website and adopt the standard boring translation agency one, which contains the following ten ingredients (in no particular order):

a)   pretty woman with headset. At least one Black or Asian person (preferably beautiful)

b)   handsome guy (any volunteers?)

c)   a firm and decisive handshake (perfect skin, sharp cuffs)

d)   lots of white teeth

e)   flags (preferably winking and waving)

f)   a dollop of smugness

g)   gleaming white background

h)   laptops everywhere

i)   a terrible mix of fonts

j)   and, above all, a whole load of ISO badges, buttons and logos which look like a bag of boiled sweets hurled in anger at the screen

A university professor responded to a quote late last night, with a couple of questions. As usual, I answered within about 5 minutes with a phone call to discuss the text.

(Top tip for the day: always pick up the phone if you have the slightest excuse to do so...)

9,000 words on the history of monasticism - perfect! When I was younger, I spent at least two of my teenage years convinced that I would one day be a monk.

Anyway, the conversation went a bit like this:

Client: That was fast!

Me: Well, we try our best.

C: So is this subject something you can handle?

M: Very much so!

C: But re payment, is it ok if I pay half today and half on the day you send it, or is that too late?

Me: No, I think that's perfectly fine.

C: And I don't want to press you, but could it be ready by the end of the month? (Today is the 13th)

M: Yes I reckon we could manage that.

C: Ok then, let's do it. There's an English book from which I quote the French version but which has to be in the original. If you can't find it, please buy it and I'll reimburse you.

M: That's fine.

C: Okay, but don't hesitate to call if you have any queries...

I KNOW you're expecting me to write 'And then I woke up.' But no, there really is such a thing as an ideal client. And

I pretty much told him so. (Top tip no 2. Clients do love a bit of praise).

There's an abbey nearby that could be the perfect place to hide away for a few days to translate this.

Except they have a strict vow of silence. Including communication with the outside world. Bit of a challenge, that.

I'll just have to make do with Gregorian Chant on a loop...

We all know about 'Things Translators Never Say'. Well here's something this translator DID say this morning to an offer of several thousand words from a client whose payments are not the world's speediest, by any stretch of the imagination.

'I'd really love to help... but my next availability will begin the day my bill is paid.'

Sometimes the simplest sentences are the best.

I may have mentioned this before, but I think it's a point worth making again. We've talked quite a bit here about luck, about opportunities and about seizing the day.

Or carping the diem if you prefer.

Now let's say you're a freelancer and you meet someone at an event. You chat, and that person (in this case, your humble correspondent) is potentially in a position to give you work.

What's more they specialise in an area which you enjoy. And to top it all, you seem to get on well.

They tell you, 'Take a look at my website, then send me your CV/portfolio and let's see.'

Now when I started out as a freelancer working with agencies, and even one or two early direct clients, I would have seen that kind of opportunity as nothing less than gold dust, and my email would have been in their inbox before they got home.

At least an initial 'Lovely to meet you... I'll get back to you asap with my details.'

So why, 4 days later, am I still waiting? (Or rather, why have I given up waiting and consider the case closed?)

Elina Sellgren *Yes, I would feel the same, even though I can think of so many situations where I intended to do something right away and then life happened. and my memory sucks ever since I lost my post it pad and haven't remembered to buy a new one. Still, it does tell you something about how important it is for someone, how quick they react.*

Standing Out *Of course, and even your heartless correspondent knows that babies can get ill, dogs get lost, a friend can call in tears. Stuff happens. But then again, how long does it take to send a one-liner? If you're inspired by what you do, you make time. It's as simple as that.*

And the prize for the most boring Dear Sir/Madam cover letter of 2014 goes to... (drumroll, opens golden envelope....)

XY of Z, during whose email I managed to doze off at least twice this morning.

I can only assume that people who write such letters find me through my website. And if you bother to spend more than, oh let's say, 3 seconds there, you'll see that I am not a Madam. Not even a little bit.

And that I don't do much Hungarian to Swahili.

And that your experience in translating fork-lift truck part catalogues is unlikely to be of much use to me.

It's better to choose one studio or agency a week and really focus your cover letter than to adopt a scattergun approach to fifty.

I know, because I did it the wrong way myself all those years ago. And of, what, 400 emails, I got perhaps 5 or 6 responses. Which in itself was lucky...

Put it this way, if you can't be bothered to spend the time finding out more and tailoring your email to the addressee, why should the addressee spend any time on you? Just a thought.

Went to a social event this evening and got talking to a posh English woman of the kind who abound in Provence. Cut-glass accent, expensive scarf, grey hair bordering on lilac.

After the opening niceties, she asked me what I did, and I said 'I'm a translator.'

She immediately interrupted and said, 'Oh, everyone's a translator down here. No money in it at all.'

Ah well, better change my job then.

Eva Hussain *I so hate patronising know it alls! Why, how and when do people become like that? As for a witty come back. Next time? Tell her you work for the CIA and they've always paid you handsomely. They're recruiting and is she interested?*

Today I got one of the biggest breaks of my translating career. Ever.

I can't tell you anything about it as it's confidential and I'd have to kill you all afterwards.

But in my mind it relates directly back to getting rid of an agency earlier in the week. Sometimes we're afraid of the vacuum that will be created if we take that plunge.

But here's another way of looking at it... what if sometimes we're carrying dead weight? I'm not talking about zippy, dynamic customers, whether agencies or direct, but that safe but lumbering client, stuck somewhere in 2004. Far from providing security, they might actually be holding you back from what you could be achieving.

Believe. Make the leap.

I'm sometimes surprised by the number of times on various fora I see someone come up with a great tip, idea, or approach, whether big or small, and at least half the people in the comments will say 'That's really, certainly, definitely and indubitably one for the to-do list.'

Well here's a confession. Even though I've downloaded at least ten to-do and list apps in bright colours and looked into enough software programmes and websites to make Bill Gates weep, I've never found one that works.

Because in the time I take to type the blasted promise into the machine, I'd usually have done the thing anyway.

So my advice is, if you see an inspiring idea, learn of an uplifting book or even come across a life-changing approach, deal with it today. Perhaps not right now, as you have a deadline to meet, a baby to feed, an executive assembly to chair or a US President to call. But still do it today.

Hildegard Klein-Bodenheimer *That reminds me of one of my favourite quotes: If Not Now, When? (Rabbi Hillel)*

A new client rang this morning, who had heard about me recently via a couple of connections that could only have come about since I started the *Standing Out* page.

Just goes to show...

We discussed a very attractive sounding text. And then they told me the length and asked my price. They were clearly used to dealing with serious prices.

I took a deep breath, thought of a nice number, bumped it up a bit, polished it a little, and then added some extra icing on top. Then I said it in as calm a voice as I could. It seemed to hover, echoing, in the air.

'That's too low,' they said.

It's hard, but sometimes you just have to swallow and raise your rate...

Life's all about sacrifices.

Today I received a text whose filename was 'Andrew'.

When you get to the point where your clients automatically and unthinkingly assign you a certain text, and even name it after you, because you're so entrenched in their processes, you know things are going OK. But never get complacent.

Treat every text as a test.

And not of the client's view of you, but of your view of you.

Today I got an email from a translator which began:

'Dear Hiring Manager'

At that point I had to make a major effort not to jump from my (2nd floor) window.

Even if I *were* a Hiring Manager, a Vendor Director or a Translation Operative Recruitment Officer, would I actually want to be *called* that?

What happened to humanity?

I'd much prefer an email that began 'Oi you idiot, listen to me!'

Eva Hussain *Also, here's a top tip for anyone who cares to listen. Most translating companies have a recruitment section on their website. Read it and follow the instructions therein. If you want to write to me (and you're welcome to, my name and contact details are on our website as well, as we try our best not to be faceless, unlike many companies) feel free to do so, just don't address me in any of the following ways:*

> *Dear Sir*
> *Dear Sir/Madam Dear Sir/Mdm Dear ,*
> *Hi ,*
> *Dear hiring manager, Dear recruitment manager*

> *No salutation at all is also a no-no. So there.*

Things not to say when applying to work with an agency, No. 245.

Just received an email today, entitled 'Ability, Accuracy, Availability'.

Yes, it's nicely balanced as a formula and looks impressive at first glance. Pretty use of assonance.

But from the other side of the desk, my immediate question is 'If you're so able and so accurate, why are you so available?'

Today I've made 5 phone calls to (direct) clients, all for questions which might conceivably have been dealt with by email.

It might not be the best approach to harried project managers at agencies (although even agencies aren't immune to the human touch!) but for direct clients it's highly recommended.

Do the maths.

There are 3.3 billion email accounts on the planet. They all use pretty much the same formulae in sending messages.

There is one person on the planet with your voice.

A call builds, cements and strengthens relationships much more effectively than an email.

So pick up the phone. Make some human contact. Isn't that what our job is about?

Ode Laforge *Ah the human voice, how wonderful indeed! Except when you hear it again and again on the answering machine of the person you decided to call instead of sending him/her an email!*

Cora Hackwith *I have worked for a translation agency where email was the norm. Thousands of emails flying around with everyone looking at everybody else's emails. Even when I took an incoming phone message for my manager (yes, the phone did ring now and again) and passed it on in person, I was told that email (2 desks away) was the preferred way of passing on messages. So my carefully written message delivered personally was not appreciated. I didn't last long.*

A specialist translator I already know but have not worked with before writes to me with a quote.

They say (from memory, and that's important... as impressions count): 'Yes I can take the text. I'll use X tool, format, translate and proofread for you to a really high quality, and all for only XXX'.

Now it so happens that XXX is more than I've ever paid to a translator in my role as a translation studio... and very nearly what I am charging the client, so we do a teensy weensy bit of negotiation, but soon settle.

But what this shows is the sheer power of confidence. When someone presents you with an upbeat case, you are almost powerless to resist.

Even when you know every trick in the book...

Wherever I look, I see blogs urging me to set goals. Short-, medium- and long-term goals. Goals for today, this year, the next 5 years and the next 50 years.

Well here's a confession. I've never set a goal in my life, apart from the daily goal of doing whatever I do to the best of my ability.

Because life, for me, has a funny habit of being totally unpredictable.

My professional presence on social media came from a chance remark by a colleague.

The *Standing Out* idea grew out of a sudden realisation that a separate Facebook page might just work.

My webinar came from an email out of the blue, following my musing online about a book I happened to read about.

I was then invited to be part of a panel for a conference in Chicago by someone I'd never heard of (but have since got to know).

Recently I got a totally unexpected phone call from a VIP offering me a lovely piece of work.

Twitter followers pop up out of nowhere and then lead to new connections.

I have no idea what's coming next. It's all gloriously haphazard and random.

For me the only golden rule is: keep your eyes open, listen, react, and leap without ever thinking too hard.

It doesn't seem to have done me too much harm so far.

In other words: be alive. The rest falls into place.

Alison Hughes *That's my philosophy too. I have a rough idea in my head where I'm going but often get side tracked by chance events.*

Heather Jennifer McCrae *Same here, just as one door slams in your face, 3 others open. My entire life has been a series of coincidences, a chance remark by someone, a sudden choice popping up, I even got into University due to the simple fact that the Professor looking at my application thought it was so amazing that I used to be a contortionist. So he called me 'just for a chat' and so on. I love the surprises in life.*

Yesterday I had to visit the doctor, for the first time since moving in December. I looked for the medical centre closest to my house, which is out in the country, and found one on the edge of the nearest town.

It was, I realised as I pulled up, in what is euphemistically called a *quartier sensible* in French. These disadvantaged housing estates are often a bit run-down, date back to the 1960s and are rather desolate, hopeless places.

The walls of the waiting room were painted dirty yellow (top half) and institutional grey (bottom). There were a dozen or so chairs, made of plastic and metal, and every one of them was broken. Either the arms were missing or the plastic coating had been ripped and the foam spilled out. A tattered poster on the wall warned of the perils of overeating.

An obese man in front of me sat with his back to the sign. When I heard the doctor's door creak open and the large man shuffled past and down the stairs, I went in.

The doctor sat there in his old cardigan, an anorak across the back of his chair. He was small, balding, and there were tufts of hair in his ears. He was surrounded by mountains of paper, envelopes, a lunchbox, three mugs on the desk, a number of opened books, cardboard boxes on the floor, two pharmaceutical company calendars (one from 2013), a flickering computer screen on a monitor which looked like it had been picked up in a car-boot sale circa 1992.

He was kindly enough and no doubt knew his medicine. Besides, luckily, my query was a simple one. But I couldn't help imagining him as a bright young student at medical school, a life of hope ahead of him. To me, he looked now like a man who had given up and was simply waiting for retirement. Or worse.

What struck me most was the fact that he clearly had no idea of the impression his surgery might make on a total newcomer. Perhaps he was just too used to his space. Perhaps he was past caring.

Our offices are not public places, it's true, but they are where we spend every day and they reflect the energy in which we work.

Does yours convey an image of dynamism or one of lassitude? In what way is the spirit in which you translate also mirrored by your surroundings?

And what would a stranger think if they walked into your space tomorrow?

Volker Freitag *A stranger would think, 'Gosh, I want to clean up this mess, but where to start?'*

It's late on Saturday night, and I've just returned from the cinema to a request for a translation quote from a serious client.

I'm delighted, and will respond right away.

But in a recent forum post, I read 'How to irritate a translator? Send them a request on a Friday evening at 7pm' or words to that effect. (Presumably the Saturday equivalent would induce an apoplectic fit).

Now I'm a little confused by this.

You see, if I was working for a regular company, then I probably *would* be a bit cheesed off to receive work just as the weekend was getting underway.

And I'd probably turn freelance as quickly as I could.

But given that I *am* a freelancer, and therefore free to respond when I want, and to say yes or no, and given that the whole point of my efforts since the beginning has been to generate work, then I'm having a little difficulty with the concept of being annoyed by job offers.

In fact, the most interesting offers from direct clients often come at unorthodox times. Because it shows that they too are working late and enjoying what they're doing.

And those kinds of clients, in my experience, are the very best people to work with.

Matt Young *Speaking as someone who has good clients in time zones from Tokyo to London to Vancouver, checking e-mails at most times of the day is just one of those necessary evils. I don't always respond instantly though, nor would my far-flung clients expect me to. By far the worst offender in terms of antisocial phone calls, however, was my grandmother during my 7 years in Japan. In her mind, if it was 8pm in Morecambe, it was 8pm everywhere on earth.*

Eva Hussain *I met the love of my life by answering the phone at 2 am. He was desperately trying to offload a big translation project and I said yes,* *promptly going back to sleep. The rest is history and kind of irrelevant here. What's important is how one treats the world around them. Cantankerous, unhelpful, patronising, negative people are not cool. Just think of last time YOU got bad customer service. Not many businesses survive by being rude. Unless you're the Soup Nazi from Seinfeld. Boundaries? By all means! As for me, I say yes to everything translation that makes money (within reason) and then work out how to do it.*

Next time someone drones on about how crowded the field is and how intense the competition, refer them to the little text in italics below. And then tell them to put it in a sandwich and eat it.

Pret opened in London in 1986. College friends, Sinclair and Julian, made proper sandwiches avoiding the obscure chemicals, additives and preservatives common to so much of the 'prepared' and 'fast' food on the market today. The two of them had woefully little experience in the world of business. They created the sort of food they craved but couldn't find anywhere else.

There are about 335 Pret shops worldwide at the moment. Most of them are in the UK and between them we turn over roughly 450 million pounds a year.

(from www.pret.com)

I was often in London in 1986, and I can guarantee you that plenty of sandwiches were available even then. So what on earth made two people dream they could not only enter the market but conquer it?

And what might be the lesson in there for translators? Because there is *always* a lesson hidden away somewhere.

We're all language pros. We all bang on about quality and perfection. And yet, and yet... I've seen quite a few sites where the English is occasionally infelicitous (to be diplomatic).

As an ex-English teacher, I think: 'Wow, you've achieved a truly outstanding level and that's amazing. Hats off. Congrats.'

As a translator I incline more towards: 'What WERE you thinking? You didn't even get it checked by a colleague??????'

It goes without saying that I had my own site translated into French by an excellent professional. I would never in a million years have dreamed of even attempting my own version.

Isn't it obvious?

Marie Jackson *I totally agree. I've spoken French since I was four, and I still wouldn't do it. You can't put a price on effective copy written by a professional who knows exactly how to make their compatriots' hearts tick!*

On the theme of how we can stand out when replying to an ad... here's a blast from the past.

September 2011, and this was my first ever ad on ProZ:

Looking to expand team of collaborators to cope with increasing workload.

If you can tick all the following boxes, write to me: Minimum 2 years' full-time

- *professional experience*
- *Able to write in a variety of styles, from tourist to business and general readership technology*
- *Ultrafast replier.*
- *Equipped with Skype, smartphone.*

These are essentials, not desirables. So please take note.

The key desirable is for you to be a generally excellent human being who likes being paid rapidly for their work.

Please send your CV and rates to me, saying something about yourself and convincing me with unassailable logic as to why I should work with you and not the others about to deluge me with their mails.

Your email must be entitled 'Translation Collaborator' for filtering purposes. Any variant thereof, including 'Translation Collaboration, Translator Collaborator' or suchlike will hit the bottom of the bin before you can say 'Instructions are important'.

Finally, only shortlisted candidates will be contacted. There will be a short (paid) test.

See below for how Alexandra Maldwyn-Davies rose to the challenge with impeccable brio… She was (following the test of course) immediately accepted, on the basis that a translation company thrives best when it has people who can translate AND have character.

Because as we all know, this is a job in which your mettle gets tested now and again.

AMD went on to become a trusted colleague over the years and has now shown such enterprise and precious mettle that she has started her own company and is thriving.

Which doesn't surprise me in the least.

Hello Andrew,

Your advert on the ProZ website sparked my interest. Please accept this letter and the attached CV as my application for collaboration projects you have at Morristraduction.

Let me briefly explain how I feel I could contribute to your agency: With over nine years' experience in translation and interpretation, I believe my qualifications will suit your requirements. I have had the opportunity to function in a variety of professional settings, making it easy to adapt to new situations and concepts.

The greatest part of my experience has been within the arts, particularly video gaming and film scripts. I have completed a large number of projects (dialogues, scripts, marketing materials, subtitling, user manuals, game rules, beta tests, web content etc). I am very much open to working in other fields. Please see my CV and ProZ profile for details of my professional background. My rates start at xxx per source word.

I would be more than happy to take your test and/or answer any questions you have about my professional experience.

I am an interesting person! I enjoy both singing and acting in my free time and have recently turned my hand to short-story writing.

I am extraordinarily fast at answering emails and have never yet missed a deadline. I thrive on them.

I am cheerful between the hours of 8.30 am and 10.30 pm, but can otherwise get quite grumpy if tired, not fed regularly enough or if I know the Tabac is closed and I only have three cigarettes left.

I try to be an excellent person. I have six rescue-cats, I give a couple of euros to a one-legged homeless woman outside the train station at least once a week and my unemployed sister has been living with me for six months and I haven't thrown her out yet.

If you are interested in a dedicated translating professional with the required credentials and positive attitude, please do not hesitate to contact me.

Thank you for taking the time to review my CV. I look forward to hearing from you.

Alexandra Maldwyn-Davies
P.S I LOVE being paid fast

Perfect mixture of key info and oddball humour. It may not work with every agency or client.

But probably more than you think.

Rob Prior *My entire business plan will be based around 'Britischer Humor'. I intend to fulfil every British stereotype there is, including appearing on my website in a bowler hat drinking a cup of tea, despite the fact I like neither hats nor tea.*

Eva Hussain *Love it! I'd hire her on the spot.*

Much ink has been spilt on the (over-)use of the word 'quality' by translators talking about their services.

'Don't state the obvious!' cry the pundits. 'Who *isn't* for quality???'

And so the Q-word, along with 'efficient', 'never missed a deadline', 'reliable' and 'accurate' are to be banished forever from the translator's lexicon.

All the same, I think we need to sort out two different audiences when we pitch our services.

a) If we're talking to other translation companies, we definitely need to carve out some new and original descriptions, as these words do tend to be overused. They're still important, but you need to find fresh ways of approaching them, interesting alternatives, similes and metaphors to evoke the same concepts.

Think laterally... diamonds, sprinters, Swiss clocks, cheetahs, Rolls Royces, blue chips. Anything in fact that carries the same cultural connotations, and play around with those when you make your pitch.

b) But for Joe Public, which includes your direct clients, I wonder in fact whether these words ARE so obvious.

To find out, I went back to my own website to see the comments written by clients and in fact, the words 'quality', 'professional', 'efficiency' and 'speed' come up time and again.

This is not about blowing my own trumpet but just to suggest that while we as translators may be tired of these words, the public is as keen as ever to use them.

And above all to experience them.

As usual at the end of the month I get all my invoices in from everyone who's translated for me.

Once they're in, I try and pay them within 24 hours. 48 tops.

It was 19 people this month. So far I have received 17 invoices. And like pretty much every month, I'll send out a reminder to a couple of people.

A reminder to be paid???

It's a funny old world. And just a little bit surreal...

To all freelancers who occasionally forget to submit bills, I'd say that money, like work, flows most easily to those who know how to manage it best.

And that if you don't master money, it will end up mastering you.

Typical Saturday morning: coffee in town followed by a trip to the organic supermarket. Service with a smile at the café, followed by an engaging chat about the idea of locavorism (eating only what's local) with the shop assistant, who was clearly inspired by what he does. So much so that a queue formed behind us to get at the apples and asparagus...

As I go about my daily life I meet a lot of people who are obviously miserable in their jobs. But what a pleasure this morning to come across two examples of the opposite category: both the waitress and the shop assistant seemed to give off a certain energy, a sense of being in the perfect job, of not wanting to be doing anything else with their lives.

Subconsciously, I tend to categorise everyone I come across. Either they have it or they don't. It's never a fixed state: those that don't have it can transform their lives, and those that have it can lose it (although that takes some effort).

Who knows the reality of the inner ups and downs of these people? But in the moment that counts: the brief encounter with a customer, they transmit a great deal of information, however unwittingly.

People who are in the zone, whether they are cleaning windows or leading a company, all have something in common. You can sense it, and it transforms everything around them. It's also infectious.

I'd probably feel more in common with an inspired shoeshine boy than with a grumpy translator.

Because there are translators in both categories too. And a few in between perhaps, chugging along. Just getting by.

124

What sense do people get of you when they talk to you about your work? What impression do you create? To which category do you belong?

Gill McKay *Of course we all want to feel in the zone as much as possible. And of course there are times when we're not. But for me at least, those times are temporary and I do my utmost not to transmit them to customers! If you're out of the zone most of the time then it's time to do something else. I agree that it makes such a difference when you have contact with people like your waitress or shop assistant. One of our local bus drivers tells jokes on the tannoy while he's driving - everyone finishes their journey with a smile on their face.*

On the joys of feedback, part 1

If ever you get feedback, even constructive feedback, you will be destabilised. It's the way we're hard-wired.

However, learning to see the gift behind the blow is vital and it's a skill that can be developed over time.

The first time I ever delivered a text with a couple of careless errors, I was rocked by the feedback.

In a split second I realised my career was over and that I would immediately have to retrain as a cosmonaut or a candlestick-maker.

It took me hours to recover.

No, no, I exaggerate. It took me days.

And even though this happened rarely (of course!) the effect was the same every time.

It was only years later that I understood the mechanism: that this was in fact free training, a great pointer and a priceless lesson in where to improve, as well as being a sign from the client that they valued you enough to invest the time in sending feedback in the first place.

Anyone who has suddenly stopped receiving work (for no apparent reason) from a client will soon come to appreciate how much better it is to receive constructive criticism...

We all have off-days and off-texts. And getting feedback will never be the most enjoyable activity. Put it alongside having your teeth drilled, being splashed with water from a passing car driving through a puddle, or listening to the sweet sound of fingernails travelling down a blackboard.

But the more you understand the mechanism, the faster you'll appreciate it.

And bounce back, ready for more.

Sara Freitas *It happens to me on average once a year or so...never pleasant but usually a good learning experience. Either that the client is a nutcase or that I didn't take time to understand their needs carefully enough, or that I quite simply did not use the most appropriate terminology for their niche...whatever the case I try to keep the best and ignore the rest.*

On the joys of feedback, part 2.

Never forget that your clients will see you as a service provider AND a human being.

But not necessarily in that order.

The other day, I translated a website for an agency, who had four quotes from clients on their 'feedback page'. And they all said pretty much the same thing: 'reliable', 'efficient', 'meets deadlines'.

Nothing wrong with that, if you're marketing yourself as a Swiss clock. Or a microwave oven.

But how much nicer it is to get feedback where they ALSO talk about you as a person... your friendliness, your flexibility or your approachability.

Similarly, the lack of such qualities can lose you both agencies and direct clients, no matter how exquisite your work might be...

So it might be worth emphasising your human side when you apply to work with agencies.

Just remember that clients have feelings too.

Just received a proofread text back from an agency I respect.

Nice to note that despite minor alterations, my face is safe from vigorous palming this happy day.

Do you often ask for texts back?

Always a sound idea when you know the proofreading team is good. (And proves your commitment of course, which is no bad thing in itself).

It can confirm your choices (giving you an excuse to celebrate with at least three pieces of chocolate) or really open up your eyes to new ways of looking at words you've often tussled with (which also go down well with chocolate, I find).

And prove of course that no two translators will ever look at the same text through the same eyes.

Been reading a rather unedifying debate about perceptions of our income.

Do people see us as low-earners?

Ask Warren Buffett. He'd probably say 'Definitely!' Ask a Bangladeshi rickshaw wallah. He'd probably compare us to Warren Buffett.

Ask *Standing Out*, and he'd probably say, 'I don't really care what either of them thinks of my earnings.'

Because, ladies and gentlemen, his main and pressing question is: does he earn enough to put olives on the table (green AND black of course)?

And the answer is yes. That's good enough for me.

Alison Hughes *Well, Champagne is my thing (although I do love olives). Only managing the odd bottle now and then but would like to think I could buy it by the case some time in the future.*

As you know I wear two hats. One is with my direct clients and the other is my work with agencies, who are permanently there, always friendly (at least the ones I work with), often flexible, occasionally forgiving and of course take some of the tiring marketing work off our shoulders...

In a quiet spell at the end of last week, I thought it was time to add a few more fresh eggs to my basket. So I went on to the Blue Board (which seems to get a bad press in some quarters but is fine if you know how to use it and are actually able to read).

My mind immediately went back to when I first started out and committed the cardinal sin of mailshooting every agency on the planet with my identical covering letter. Despite the fact that I thought it was devastatingly witty and elegant... it still seemed to go down like a lead balloon.

Maybe humour doesn't travel that easily after all... Maybe it's just my humour.

Or maybe it was just the wrong approach.

Anyway, 458 applications later, I received about 8 answers, 4 of which turned into concrete contacts, all of which are still with me. Not bad, you might think, but it was still a pretty dismal 1% record overall.

Built up a couple more over time, got rid of a few too, so never totalled more than say, seven at once, with two or three star agencies in near daily contact.

Now being older, wiser, more confident and with a dinky website under my belt, (plus my CV and portfolio all ready of course) I decided to try something different, to call and give them my spiel live, along the lines of: 'Are you looking to strengthen your team with a really good translator in the x and y fields?'

Surprisingly enough, no-one said no.

I sent off 6 follow-up emails and got 6 answers. That's a 100% record. Something of an improvement, *n'est-ce pas*?

So pick up the phone, show your vitality and never despatch a timid enquiring email again.

Use your voice. Stand out.

I've often wondered exactly what place we occupy in a client's hierarchy of contacts.

Take Béatrice (not her real name). She works as a communications manager at a major museum that stages some serious international exhibitions. So exactly how many people are in her address book? Sponsors great and small of course, experts and academics for all those exhibition texts, audio guide recording studios, graphic designers, printers and kakemono makers, not to mention the caterers, florists and local dignitaries for launches and gala evenings.

And somewhere amongst all that is your humble servant, the translator.

It's enough to make you realise what a tiny cog you are. Enough, at times, to make you hesitate in reaching for the phone, so as not to bother busy Béa with a question.

And yet, the very day Béa leaves her job, amongst all the welter of things that clearing a desk involves, amidst all the doubts and insecurities and tears and farewells (or conversely sighs of relief and whoops of joy?), she finds time to write this unsolicited note:

'Ca a toujours été un grand plaisir de travailler avec vous, pour votre rapidité, votre professionnalisme et votre gentillesse, et je n'hésiterai pas à faire appel à vous de nouveau si j'en ai l'occasion dans mes prochains postes.' [6]

It's then that you understand that it doesn't matter how far down the client's list you are, (and it might be less far down than you think) your job is to always treat them as though they are at the very top of yours.

And sooner or later, it all comes around.

Zoe Beal *Absolutely. For me, it's 'simply' a question of doing as I would be done by in all walks of life, really, being courteous, respectful and obliging - as well as being the very best professional person and translator that I possibly can. So far, I've experienced nothing but the same in return.*

Allison Klein Kruter *Excellent. And one of the PMs that left an agency I used to do a lot of work for has been in the publishing industry ever since, and now sends me book translations.*

Peter Bowen *Also an object lesson in how to treat your own suppliers. A kind word or simply any feedback of any kind never goes amiss. There is too little of it in our professional sphere.*

---

6 *It's always been a great pleasure to work with you, for your speed, professionalism and kindness, and I'll certainly call on your services again if I get a chance in my future jobs..."*

Hildegard Klein-Bodenheimer *I believe, with all the frustrations and rantings in translator land, we (the translators) often forget that clients are grateful for our work, that they know what they would miss if we were not there, and that they appreciate our efforts and the diligence in our work. And I am sure that a communications manager at a major museum knows the importance of quality. So, here is to good clients!*

When the phone rang from a magazine client in Germany this week, my brain smiled as it saw the number display on the handset. That could only mean more work.

However, when the secretary said 'The editor would like a word', those same grey cells experienced a slight moment of panic.

Why is it that a part of me always expects the worst? That's quite an achievement for a born optimist…

Had I missed a semi-colon or mistranslated a word? Had I forgotten a paragraph or got an idiom horrendously wrong? Even as the drawbridge of my braincastle was lowered in anticipation of the editor coming on the line and the trumpeters lined up in the courtyard, the archers scrambled and took up positions on the parapet, ready to defend my honour just in case. But in the end, they had an easy time of it, as the editor had just wanted to praise a translation, not to bury it.

The title of a section in the magazine all about the ice rinks amid the Christmas markets in many German cities had been

'Glatteis Willkommen!*'* which translates literally as 'Sheet Ice Welcome'.

Not much of a headline in English, I'm sure you'll agree. In fact, it's a load of sheet.

So I toyed around for a while, tried 'An Icy Welcome' but soon came to my senses: that is in fact the opposite of what a tourist is looking for.

Until I hit upon the solution that delighted the editor so much....

'What an ice welcome!' Result: one happy client.

Wrote to an agency with my usual email signature containing the picture of the golden egg, which links to my website.

I get so bored with reading the carbon-copy Dear Sir/ Madam letters sent to me that I thought I'd send a message with a difference.

It just said:

'I could send you my CV but that wouldn't tell you much. Take a look at my website by clicking on the marvellous golden egg below, and if you like what you see in terms of experience, specialist areas and presentation values, drop me a line and let's talk.'

Result? They replied immediately.

Try it some time. With your own eggs of course.

Recently I've started adding phrases like 'And don't hesitate to tell others about our services!' when writing back to satisfied clients or speaking to them on the phone.

Of course it probably happens anyway in some cases, but we all know how powerful word of mouth is, and a little reminder can't do any harm...

The more energy you inject into your communications, the further it'll carry you...

A client asks me for a 30-word translation for a brochure cover.

'Do you need it by Monday afternoon?' quoth I.

'No, any time next week is fine... Whenever you can.'

Oh happy days.

Politeness costs nothing, even when a company is obviously a bit on the bogus side. I got an email which looked quite interesting just now from an agency... that is until I looked at their results on the ProZ Blue Board, which were characterised by a whole series of ones.

Inspired by the spirit of client education, I snipped and copied a selection of said onesies and sent the following message:

'Many thanks for your mail.

I understand your message is in good faith, but your reputation as a company unfortunately precedes you.

Please see attachment. Best wishes'

After all, it's not the PM's fault…

For many translators, the distinction between premium and bulk markets has provided an innovative, eye-opening and welcome new categorisation.

These two labels, with their strong value-laden connotations, have given practitioners a dual gift: they now know both what they have to steer clear of and what they can aspire to.

'Bulk' clearly refers to the behemoths around the world that churn out words by the million rather than the thousand, or the many low-paying agencies, while 'premium' describes the blue-chip companies and top-end clients who tend to gather around the finance and business districts of the world's capitals, as well as in the luxury sector.

The two terms have since entered the translation discourse mainstream and are widely used in online discussions. Everyone now knows that bulk is bad and premium is priceless. And of course it's a perfectly clear and valid division.

As far as it goes.

Because I think there's something missing from the picture, which offers a slightly polarised view. Let's call the path between the two extremities the Middle Way. Alas, I can't claim to have coined the term, which appears to have been first invented by a Mr G. Buddha around 5,000 years ago, but it will serve us well enough here.

No freelancer in their right mind wants to be caught up in the bulk machine, unless for some obscure reason they've made their peace with low pay in return an easy(?) and predictable life. But whether every freelancer capable of producing polished work is able to get a foot in the door of the premium market right away is another question altogether.

By its very definition, the premium market is an exclusive niche and usually accessible only if you live near the national or even international centres of power.

It's also a highly rarefied sanctum in terms of talent. To operate at that level, you need to have earned your spurs over the years, if not decades. And you need to be not just polished but sparkling. It's a goal we can and should aspire to, but many of us are not quite there yet. Don't rush it: it's a step-by-step process.

However, that still leaves plenty of rich pickings for the enterprising freelancer in the meanwhile.

When I peruse my client list for 2014, there's not a blue-chip company in sight, but there are plenty of small and medium-sized firms, often with small and medium-sized budgets, who nevertheless invest no less passion and commitment in their texts than the CEOs of major enterprises in the capital.

There's a museum (state-funded), an airline magazine publisher, an artisanal ice-cream manufacturer, an art gallery, a handful of communications agencies, a successful DJ, a property developer, a regional TV company, a camping holiday company, a bike tourism outfit, a research institute, a small arty publishing house and a sprinkling of university academics.

None of them fits the word premium as I understand it (unless 'premium' is merely a synonym for 'direct', which would make it redundant) but all are deeply committed to their texts and all pay a healthy rate for direct translation work.

My communication with these clients usually involves one sole interlocutor, to whom I turn for all matters, from quotes to queries to invoices, frequently involving phone conversations. The relations vary from cordial (at the very minimum) to positively back-slapping, and naturally from my point of view, they all get the same treatment and speed of response as would Bill Gates if he were on the other end of the line.

We found each other through a variety of methods: business events and conferences, random meetings, targeted messages sent on the off-chance offering my services, word-of-mouth referrals, the occasional answer to an ad, my Facebook page or simply by being visible on Google.

Some new prospects fall by the wayside of course: not every quotation I send out is accepted, but there's certainly enough translation work to keep olives on the table and indeed to have established a business which at times has outsourced to several freelancers each month.

So between the dreaded treadmill of the bulk sector and the shimmering golden city of the premium markets, there are in fact thousands of small clients, each devoted to their projects, and most of whom would be only too happy to work with a skilled freelancer like you... if only they knew one. And you'd be all the more attractive if you could team up with someone to proofread your work and therefore guarantee an impeccable end product.

So don't focus your gaze on the murky depths. But don't crane your neck too much by looking too far up to the glittering heights either. All in good time.

Meanwhile, just look around, and occupy the middle ground.

Where there's plenty of room for all of us.

First published in the ITI Bulletin

6 LOOSE ENDS

A skinny cat stood for hours waiting for the mouse to venture out from behind its hole, so he could nab him. He was having little success. A fat cat walked by, inquired about the nature of the difficulty, and volunteered to show the skinny cat the ropes. First thing, he had the skinny cat move out of the way where he could not be seen and did likewise himself. Next, he barked, 'Woof, woof.' The mouse, thinking a dog had scared the cat away and it was safe, ventured out only to be devoured by the fat cat. 'You see,' explained the fat cat, 'it pays to be bilingual.'

Of course these days the skinny cat would have used Google Translate and the mouse, spotting a bogus translation, would have lived to eat another cheese...

Working on translation of a paper by an academic who has spent his entire professional life researching voodoo dolls. But not in Haiti, or Brazil, but Western Europe. And not any old European voodoo dolls, but specifically those of the 5th/6th centuries BCE. Crudely fashioned, often filled with tiny seeds so that they rattle. Used to cast spells, render enemies impotent, ruin a business competitor.

Could be useful for translators?

First job of the day, proofreading a brochure for the luxury French ski resort of Courchevel. Prices begin at 32,000 euros per square metre. Tempted, anyone?

Maybe we could all work for a year, then club together and buy a door handle.

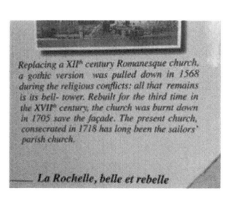

Replacing a XIIth century Romanesque church, a gothic version was pulled down in 1568 during the religious conflicts: all that remains is its bell- tower. Rebuilt for the third time in the XVIIth century, the church was burnt down in 1705 save the façade. The present church, consecrated in 1718 has long been the sailors' parish church.

— La Rochelle, belle et rebelle

La Rochelle may be 'belle et rebelle'
But its local translators don't do so well

A missed capital here, an extra space there
Why is it that people just don't seem to care?
Using Roman numerals for dates is just daft...
In future get someone who's proud of their craft!
It may be expensive, but well worth the fee
In fact, next time, why not contact me!

What do you reckon? Shall I send them my poem, or just sit back and wait for the Nobel Prize for Literature?

My colleague Mr Zhang was an owlish, bespectacled man. Shy, softly-spoken, and like everyone else in Xi'an in 1988, always dressed in a navy Mao suit.

One day over dinner he told me of how years earlier he had left China to do a Master's in Edinburgh.

Now you may not know this, but Chinese people never hug. Not friends, not families. And they don't kiss on the cheek either. Things may be changing now, but back then it was certainly a culture in which shows of intimacy (outside of a couple) were considered highly embarrassing.

Mr Zhang's father had accompanied him to the airport, about to see his son leave for a whole two years. And just as the flight was announced, he suddenly lunged forward and took his son in his arms.

Even recounting the story, Mr Zhang looked discomfited. This was simply unheard of. When I asked him how he'd reacted, he said that he'd stood as stiff as a board, utterly immobile and certainly unable to reciprocate. He boarded the plane and left for distant Scotland.

He never saw his father again. The old man died six months later.

And for the rest of his life, Mr Zhang regretted his conventional vision, his hidebound beliefs and his inability to seize the day.

Sentence of the day (thankfully from an editing piece rather than a translation):

'The first tool we use to process margin sequences is the edit distance, defined as a normalised weighted Levenshtein distance adapted to the case of a vectorial alphabet, close to the edit distance with real penalty (Chen and Ng, 2004).'

Three thoughts:

a) Isn't it amazing how we end up in such wonderfully different fields?

b) Imagine Chen, Ng and Levenshtein in primary school in (let's say) Shanghai, Hanoi and New York, all going through a pretty similar initial schooling. Did they know what lay ahead, even then? Did their young hearts skip a beat when they had their first glimpse of algebra?

c) What on earth does the edited sentence mean? (Only joking).

If you could go back to any period prior to the 20th century and be a translator, which would you choose, and why?

What would be the joys and the challenges?

I could easily see myself as a mediaeval monk, translating from Latin into the vernacular, with the sound of Gregorian Chant filling the air, the feel of the parchment under my fingers, and a well-stocked library across the cloister.

Not so keen on mead and the diet in the Middle Ages though. And no coffee of course...

And Brigitte? Well she'd be in the convent just down the road, just over the wall, so no worries there...

I never said I'd be a well-behaved monk...

Heather Jennifer McCrae *I hardly think many women would want to go back to before the 20th century. With our knowledge, we would all be classed as witches and you know what happened to them! No thanks, I am happy here, in fact, I wish I could be born again in about 100 years, just to see what has happened in the future! But this is a good time to be in.*

Joao Correia *I guess the dark ages, 1100 onward, because of incunabula, which are just amazing pieces.*

Andrzej Michalik *And draughts ventilating your privates because underwear hasn't been invented yet. The lice, the bedbugs, the smell of roasting witches ...*

Going to start on a 6,000 word piece today using Dragon. Yesterday I dictated more of my book and because I have a wireless headset, I could walk around my office, gesticulating to my heart's content. Luckily there was no-one in a white coat to lock me up.

But stop a moment and imagine a visitor from the past, even *my* past, circa 1964, (when the whole world was in black and white of course) and what they would have made of:

1) a man talking to himself wearing a headset with a mic attached
2) a keyboard (two keyboards, with no wires!)
3) a colourful screen with words appearing on it out of thin air
4) the fact that via that screen I could chat to people everywhere
5) the fact that those people's faces could appear on the screen at the touch of a button
6) the fact that music appears to be playing from a second screen
7) a machine that seems to make coffee
8)

Now imagine 50 years into the future. I may still be here. You too...

What machines will people be using then, which we haven't even dreamed of? Any futurologists amongst you? What's round the corner?

Makes the mind boggle...

The first time I came across email was back in 1997, when studying for my Master's in Education in England. I'd never been on the Internet either, and I can remember thinking 'Pah! Who needs this thing when we are surrounded by libraries?' I thought the same about e-books and was even quite late in getting a mobile phone.

Anyway, back then, we had frequent questions and often went to the College's nerve centre, the IT department.

The arch-IT-wizard was a very geeky long-haired guy in glasses. Think John Lennon, but almost always in a black heavy metal t-shirt. He sat in his dimly-lit room surrounded by monitors and cables, and usually looked like he needed a good dose of sunshine and some fresh vegetables to perk him up.

One day I went there early with a query and he booted up his computer. As the screen came to life, it greeted him with the message 'Good morning Overlord, I am here to obey you.'

What message would you like your computer to say to you this morning?

Heather Jennifer McCrae *'Good morning, Heather, I checked your work list and translated the work for you ready to proofread, ordered the weekly shop, activated the household robots and switched on the coffee machine.'*

In my inbox this morning:

Hello! Vendor Manager,

This is YF from Transpac. please contact me directly for any collaboration projects if any. So sorry to trouble you, may I know if we could provide some helps for you this year?

[...]

I guarantee delivery at the due time as I never missed my due time.

I know it's one that we all get, but it made me smile all the same.

1) They clearly don't know I don't manage vendors. (My vendors are totally unmanageable for a start)
2) 'So sorry to trouble you'? That's what we say when we go to the neighbour for a cup of sugar.
3) 'May I know?' Weird. Not English.
4) 'Provide some helps.'?? Even weirder.
5) 'Due time'? Are you expecting a boy or a girl? Tempted to reply:

Dear YF

I do love helps. Especially when they're countable. Some days I need as many helps as I can. I'm sure that your helps will also bring me lots of happinesses.

Oh and good luck with the delivery.
Hugs and kisses
Andrew

Doing a text about Teutonic pilgrims bound for Jerusalem... in 1190.

Imagine the travel conditions. The days and days on horseback... the inns where they stayed. What they ate by candlelight, the horses neighing outside under the stars.

And who did the translation when they came across other pilgrims?

Imagine their state of mind, the romances and the feuds... and how they must have felt when they finally arrived and saw the towers and spires on the horizon.

Hard times.

But at least they avoided being patronised by spotty teenagers on low-cost airlines.

Peter Bowen *Once there, did they bag the best loungers before the British pilgrims?*

Standing Out *The British pilgrims queued politely.*

Ode Laforge *Romances? I wonder how much opportunity they had to meet women. In inns I imagine, where comely maidservants would serve them drinks, and probably act as translators too, being frequently in contact with clients of many different origins. Enough to start a romance, I guess!*

Joao Correia *All in all they were happy folk and you know it: there were no taxes, no proofreaders, no calls at 7 pm on a Friday to be in Jerusalem on Sunday by noon sharp and there was no Google Translator. Bliss. Pure bliss.*

Susanne Heizmann *'What they ate by candlelight'... they probably never knew. And were eaten by bedbugs at night - I definitely prefer living today, with decent heating and hollow-fibre bedding.*

Anna Barbosa *I immediately saw myself dressed as a boy, riding a donkey on my way to the Holy Land with my master... I, the very savvy language expert, invited by a very famous historian (and fully supported as to my disguise), eager to learn ever more but unaware of the perils yet to be met... Great way to start the week: adventure mood full throttle!*

Imagine you walk into your neighbourhood bar, café, bookshop or park and to your sheer astonishment, you bump into you.

But the other you is not who you are now but who you were on the very first day you became a translator. Your younger you tells the present you about their (your) plans for the future.

As usual, however, your younger you is in a hurry, and time is short...

So if you could offer just one brief piece of advice, what would it be?

Marie Jackson *It's not so much a case of going too fast, but trying to go at an impossible pace and achieve everything all at once. We all only have 24 hours in a day and you can't do everything. I spent maybe a year feeling very frustrated that I wasn't doing EVERYTHING before my mother finally got through to me on that one.*

Allison Wright *Keep going. You're going to be fabulous when you're fifty, kid!*

This afternoon I went to the annual village dictée (dictation) in which we all sit in rows like at school, while a local poet reads out a text designed in every way to trip people up, full of slang expressions, outlandish phrases, and a mystery right to the end as to the gender of the main protagonist, which of course changes everything in French. Plus lashings of past subjunctives, classical allusions and other man-traps.

The dictation itself runs to about 3 pages... We were about 40 in all. And I was the only foreigner.

I came 4th! (The mayor came 5th). Yaay. And I won a magnum of rosé wine.

So now you see, children, why it pays to study your French grammar at school...

Wandering through the online world of translation makes me think at times of a mediaeval scene.

Movement everywhere, bustling crowds, a clamorous din. Around the busy marketplace, where coins and notes change hands, some sell silk while others deal in leather or cloth. Goblets overflowing with mead are raised.

Amid the hubbub, there are doctors selling the latest cures, knife-grinders, jugglers, hucksters, entertainers, drunkards, sages and lunatics. While up behind the mullioned windows toil the quiet scholars, learned teachers and dedicated scribes.

Over in the corner are the villains in the stocks, being pelted with rotten apples.

A noose swings from the gallows. But today it hangs empty.

There are bombastic priests and pious nuns preaching the end of days. Once in a while, a bishop glides by in a stately carriage, or an aristocrat on their way to a joust amid the outlying fields.

And right there by the fountain sits the village idiot, watching, noting, knowing that there is nothing new under the sun.

And that all things will pass.

Peter Bowen *Sounds remarkably like Brixton Market*

Rob Prior *And then everyone dies from plague. Yep sounds familiar.*

Hildegard Klein-Bodenheimer *I found that type of market in Morocco in 1995, including a barber pulling the teeth of the market goers, showing us a tin bowl with maybe 20 bloody teeth by noon. At that time, they offered my husband 12 camels for our daughter (8 years old), he refused heroically.*

I had my Dragon Naturally Speaking on when the cleaner came into the room.

I forgot to turn it off and answered a question (in French of course).

When I turned back to my screen, I saw this:

'And the work is the bubble gum litter on the Dom with a commendable good meal lavish.'

Pure poetry! *Au fond, je suis un lyrique...*

But what did I actually say? Can't remember for the life of me …

Amid all this talk of balance, keeping calm and equanimity, perhaps it's just as well you couldn't see *Standing Out* at around 7pm last night when his computer refused to boot up after crashing.

Funnily enough, I can stay calm in all kinds of human confrontations and my dissolving approach has worked pretty well up till now over 5 years of dealing with clients, translators, mini-crises, late deliveries, non-deliveries, jobs imploding, the occasional complaint etc, etc.

But once technology gives up on me, something inside goes ballistic and all I want to do is take a mallet to the computer and smash it into a million tiny fragments.

I guess it's because it's totally beyond my control. Once a computer doesn't do exactly what I paid it to do the day I bought it, I either shout uselessly or sit in a sort of paralysis. And in this mode, my imagination is easily ignited: within two seconds I see all the texts I won't be able to do, the money I'll lose, plus the money I'll now have to fork out of course for a new desktop and all the problems that will be set off from now till the end of time.

Anyway, thank goodness for her Brigitteness. Calm, rational and generally an excellent human being, she had me phone a computer repair guy who turned out to be delightful, and went way beyond the call of duty in giving me patient instructions down the phone, until all was well again. Definitely a new entry for my address book.

So the sense of balance was restored, I made a new contact and my boundless admiration for my partner only grew.

Problem dissolved.

It just took a while, that's all.

Hey, life's a learning journey. I didn't say I'd arrived yet!

Emeline Jamoul *Isn't it also due to our times though? I have the feeling that we're growing more and more impatient due to the nature of Internet and technology. We want everything NOW.*

Peter Bowen *There is probably a term for the strength of frustration based on the level of dependence on the device in question. We depend absolutely on our PCs for our livelihood. Hence the level of frustration. When my electric nose hair clipper fails, I can resort to (more painful) alternatives.*

Standing Out *Totally agree. Same goes for my electric potato peeler.*

And finally…

Family lore has it that when I was a baby I never spoke. No 'ma'. no 'ga'. Not even so much as a 'da'.

So much so that my parents thought I was not quite normal. Incidentally, it's a conclusion from which they have never really wavered, but that's another story.

They took me to the family doctor, who managed to allay their fears, but young Morris (1964, Beatlemania in its infancy, the whole scene in black and white of course) still refused to speak.

For those who think I talk too much now, there's your answer. Just making up for lost time.

And then, on my second birthday on 31st August 1966, I said the words 'Happy Birthday'. Just like that. Obviously an early horror of making mistakes, wanting to get it right…

I heard the story so often in the family it sort of slipped by unnoticed after a while. It was only recently that my dear Brigitte pointed out that, in fact, the real point had gone unremarked: that my first ever word was 'Happy'.

Now I don't know about you, but I quite like that...

If you wish to be kept up to date with all the latest from Standing Out, please write to Andrew Morris at standingout@morristraduction.com so that you can be added to the news list.

154

Printed in Great Britain
by Amazon